The Activity Bible

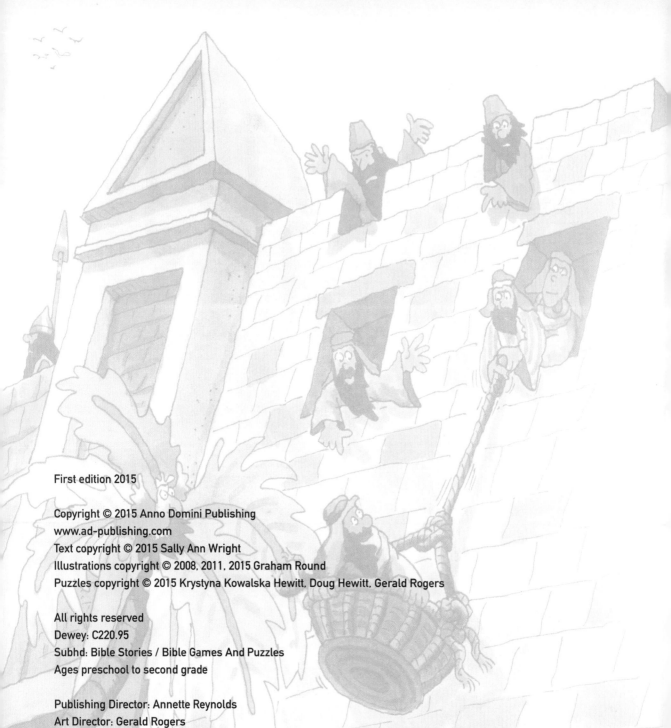

First edition 2015

Copyright © 2015 Anno Domini Publishing
www.ad-publishing.com
Text copyright © 2015 Sally Ann Wright
Illustrations copyright © 2008, 2011, 2015 Graham Round
Puzzles copyright © 2015 Krystyna Kowalska Hewitt, Doug Hewitt, Gerald Rogers

Dewey: C220.95
Subhd: Bible Stories / Bible Games And Puzzles
Ages preschool to second grade

Publishing Director: Annette Reynolds
Art Director: Gerald Rogers
Pre-Production Manager: Krystyna Kowalska Hewitt

Printed in China

The Activity Bible

52 Weeks of Stories, Puzzles, and Activities

Stories by Sally Ann Wright
Illustrations by Graham Round

BH
KIDS

EVERY *little* WORD MATTERS
BHKidsBuzz.com

Contents

The Old Testament

The New Testament

The Old Testament

God Makes a World

Genesis 1:1–31

At the beginning of time, the world was dark and empty.

Then God spoke into the darkness.

"Let there be light!" He commanded.

Light appeared, and God was pleased with what He saw. He made day and night to separate the light and the darkness.

God made sky above the earth. He made huge mountains, valleys, and rolling hills. He made the deep blue sea.

God made plants and flowers and trees with juicy fruit, prickles, and leaves. He made wheat, barley, and oats.

God made stars in the sky. He made planets, the red-hot sun, and the silvery moon.

Then came an exciting moment! God filled the sea with slippery, shiny fish and the air with birds that chatter and sing. God made animals that leap and clamber and crawl on the land.

God was pleased with everything He had made. It was good.

"Now I will make human beings," said God. "They will look after the world I have made and all the animals in it. They will eat the juicy fruit and the ripe grain of the fields."

God made the first man and called him Adam. He took some soil and blew the breath of life into Adam. Then He made a woman, called Eve, to be Adam's companion.

God wanted Adam and Eve to enjoy His world. He wanted them to be happy. God loved them very much. He made a beautiful garden for them to live in. It was called the garden of Eden.

God looked at all He had made and was pleased with His creation. It was a very good world.

SPOT the DIFFERENCES

There are ten differences between the two pictures below.
Can you circle each of them?

COLOR by NUMBERS

Use the numbers below to make the butterfly beautiful.

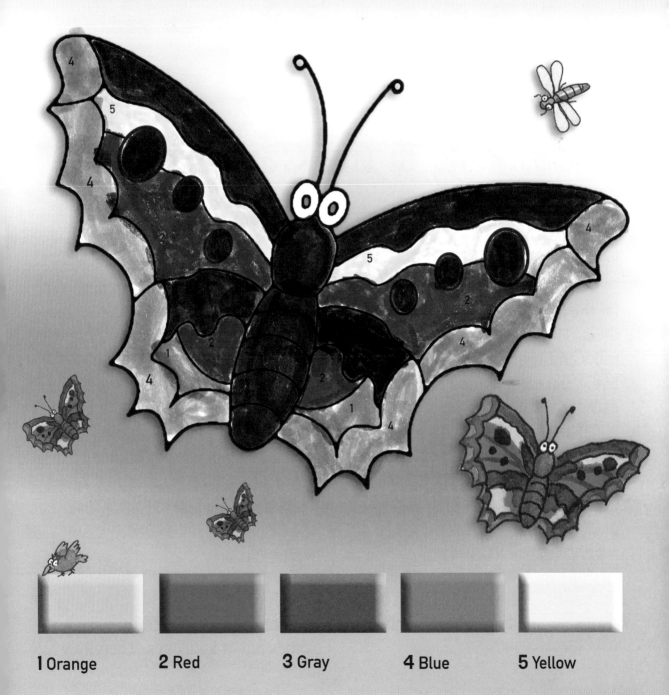

1 Orange   **2** Red   **3** Gray   **4** Blue   **5** Yellow

The Enemy in the Garden

Genesis 2:8—3:24

Adam and Eve were very happy living in the beautiful garden.

God asked them to choose names for the animals and to take care of them. The garden was full of delicious fruits and vegetables, and Adam and Eve could eat anything they wanted, except the fruit from one tree.

There was a big tree in the middle of the garden. Before God made Eve, he told Adam about it. "It is called the tree of knowing good and bad. You mustn't eat any of its fruit. If you do, everything will be spoiled."

One day, God's enemy came into the garden. He wanted to spoil all the things God had made and planned.

In the form of a serpent, the enemy crept up to Eve and hissed in her ear.

"God was lying when He told you about that tree. You won't die if you eat its fruit. You will be great, just like God! You will know all that He knows."

Eve looked at the tree. The fruit looked so delicious. She took a big, deep bite. Then she gave some to Adam.

Suddenly they knew what they had done. They didn't feel the same any more.

Everything was spoiled. They had disobeyed God.

Adam and Eve made themselves clothes out of fig leaves. Then they hid.

When God came to the garden to talk to His friends, He called out to them.

"Where are you?"

But Adam and Eve were afraid to talk to God. They felt guilty because they had disobeyed Him. Then they tried to blame each other.

God was very sad.

"Because you did not trust Me," He told them, "you will have to leave the beautiful garden. We can no longer walk and talk together as friends."

So Adam and Eve had to leave the Garden of Eden and did not return.

COLOR the DOTS

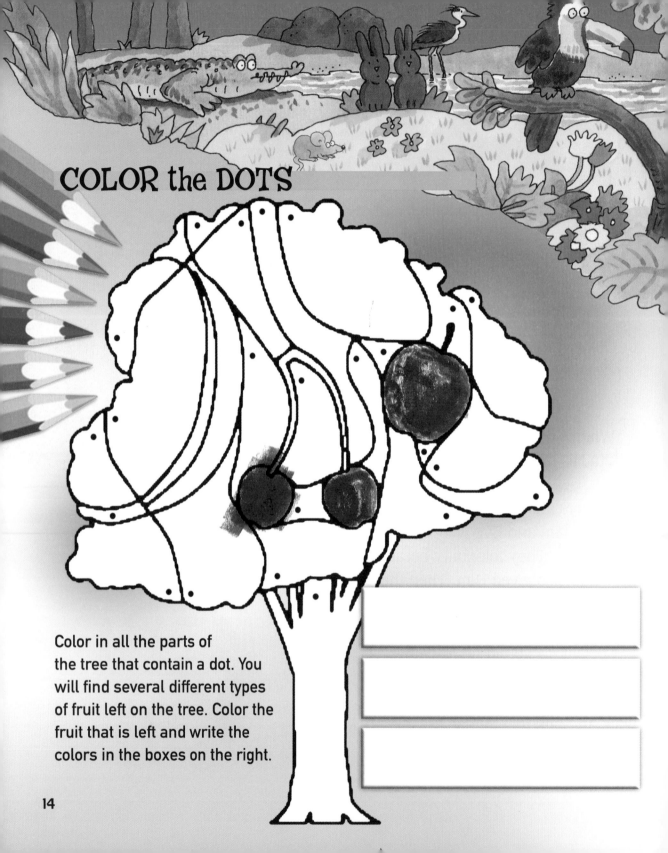

Color in all the parts of the tree that contain a dot. You will find several different types of fruit left on the tree. Color the fruit that is left and write the colors in the boxes on the right.

FIND and COUNT

Count how many times each of these things appears in the picture of the garden where everything goes wrong.

Write your answers in the boxes.

A 4

B 7

C 1

D 2

Noah's Ark
Genesis 6:9–7:24

God was sad. The beautiful world He had made was ruined. People were fighting each other and becoming more and more evil.

There was only one good man left. He was called Noah. He had a wife and three grown-up sons—Shem, Ham, and Japheth.

God spoke to Noah. "I will destroy the people on the earth! But I promise to save you and your family. This is how you will be safe: you must build a large boat from wood. Make it a triple-decker with a door at the front. Coat it with tar to keep out the water. I am going to flood the earth!

"Take into the boat all your family and pairs of every kind of animal on the earth. We will keep them alive. Take food for your family and the animals."

Noah did as God told him and built a huge triple-decker boat.

Noah was six hundred years old when the flood came. He and his family went into the boat, along with a male and female of every kind of animal and bird.

Then God shut the door.

The rain began to fall, and the earth was flooded. The boat floated on the waters.

"Hold on tight, everybody!" shouted Noah. "And don't panic! God will keep us safe!"

SHAPES

Name these five animal shapes.

Giraff

PENGUiN

WORD SEARCH

The names of all the animals in the pictures are hidden in the grid of letters below. Put a line through each of them as you find them.

owl

dog

a	g	h	p	w	v
l	i	o	n	x	a
f	m	r	p	i	g
o	a	s	m	d	a
x	p	e	o	w	l
d	o	g	v	w	m

horse

pig

lion

fox

Rain, Rain, and More Rain

Genesis 8:1—9:17

It rained and rained and rained. It rained like it had never rained before. The earth was flooded. There was nothing left to see. No trees, no fields, no houses, no people. It had all been washed away.

Noah and the animals were safe in the boat. They had enough food to last them for a long time.

"I wonder when the rain will stop?" asked one of Noah's sons. "Surely this can't go on for very much longer!"

Then God made a strong wind blow, and the water on the earth began to go down. The rain stopped. It took a hundred and fifty days for the water to run back into the soggy ground.

Noah waited for the boat to come to rest on a bit of land. There was nothing in sight at first. Nothing but water all around. Then at last the mountaintops appeared!

Noah sent a raven out of the boat. It flew round and round until the water had gone down. Noah sent out a dove, but it found no place to rest and flew back to Noah. A week later Noah sent the dove out again. This

time it returned with an olive branch in its beak. It had found a tree!

At last, God called Noah, saying, "Leave the boat, you and your family and all the animals. Fill the land with the birds and animals. Have children and fill the entire earth again."

God put a beautiful rainbow in the sky, a huge stripy archway of red, orange, yellow, green, blue, indigo, and violet. Noah and his family had never seen anything so wonderful.

"This rainbow is a sign of My promise," God said. "I will never again destroy all living things on the earth with a flood. I make this promise to you and to all living things on the earth."

ELEPHANT in the MAZE

Now that all the animals have come out of the ark, can you help the elephant to find its mate?

START

MATCHING PARTS

Draw a line to connect the correct back and front of as many of the animals below as possible.

How many animals can be completed?

Abram Moves to Canaan

Genesis 12:1–8

A long time after the time of Noah, when people had again begun to live on the land and make their homes there, God spoke to a man called Abram.

"I want you to leave your home and your country. Leave behind the people you grew up with and the land that belonged to your father. I want you to go to a land that I will show you. I will bless you there and make a great nation from your family."

Abram believed God. He was not a young man. He was already seventy-five years old. But he set off with his wife, Sarai, and his nephew, Lot. They had lots of servants and lots of camels and donkeys, sheep, and goats. They

packed up everything they had and started their long journey. They didn't know exactly where they were going, and they didn't know how long it would take, but Abram trusted God to take him to a land he could make his home.

God took Abram and his family to the land of Canaan, a beautiful land good for growing food and grazing their flocks of sheep and goats. They passed by a holy place called Shechem where there was a special tree called Moreh.

"This is the land that I am going to give to you and your people," God told Abram.

Abram built an altar there to the Lord. He moved southwards to the hills near Bethel and pitched his tents there to make it his home.

SHEEP SIZES

Abram had many sheep in his flock.
Can you put a **B** on the biggest sheep
and an **S** next to the smallest?

How many sheep
can you count?

COLOR the PICTURE

Color in the clothes of Abram and Sarai to complete the picture.

Baby Isaac

Genesis 15:4–5; 17:4–16; 18:1–15; 21:1–3

Abram believed God's promise to bless him, but Abram and Sarai still had no children.

"Look at the stars, and try to count them!" God said to Abram. "You will have as many descendants as there are stars in the sky."

God changed Abram's name to Abraham and Sarai's name to Sarah as a sign that God would give them a son.

One day, Abraham looked up and saw three men standing there. "Let me bring you some water!" said Abraham. "Come and rest here a while. I will bring some food for you."

Abraham hurried off to find Sarah.

"Quick! We have visitors!" he said. "Bake some bread!" Then Abraham ran to find the best calf in his herd and told a servant to prepare it. He took the food and served it to his visitors.

"Where is your wife?" asked one of the men.

"She is still in the tent," said Abraham.

"Nine months from now she will be nursing your son," said the visitor.

Sarah laughed to herself. "I am far too old for that!" she whispered.

But God was listening and said to Abraham, "Is anything too hard for Me? Sarah will indeed have a son."

Sure enough, nine months later, Sarah gave birth to baby Isaac.

Isaac brought great joy to his parents. He was a true gift from God.

Isaac grew up and married a beautiful girl called Rebecca. They had twin boys, Jacob and Esau. Abraham was their proud grandfather! God had kept His promise.

FIND the MATCH

Which of these four pictures matches the picture of Sarah below?

Check the box to show the match.

| 1 | 2 | 3 | 4 |

HOW MANY?

How many types of animals can you see?

STAR PUZZLE

How many stars can you count in this picture?

Circle the star that is different in shape.

Jacob Plays a Trick

Genesis 25:21–34; 27:1–45

Isaac's twin boys, Esau and Jacob, were quite a handful!

Even when they were inside their mother's tummy, they had jumped about and struggled against each other! Esau had been born first. He was red and hairy all over. He grew up to love hunting and being outdoors. Jacob was born second, and he came out holding tightly to his brother's heel! Jacob had smooth skin. He liked staying at home with his mother, Rebecca.

Esau was his father's favorite. One day, Esau would get his father's special blessing and all his riches. Jacob was his mother's special son.

One day, Esau came in from hunting and was very hungry. "I'd give anything for some of that soup!" he told his brother, Jacob.

Jacob had a cunning plan. "You can have some if you give me your rights as the firstborn son!"

"Oh all right, just give me some soup!" said Esau. Jacob smiled a cunning smile. He was now going to be the one to get all his father's riches one day.

Father Isaac grew old and blind. One day he called for his son, Esau.

"My son, Esau, I am old. I might die one day soon. Go hunting and cook me some of that tasty food I like. Then I will give you my final blessing."

Rebecca was listening at the door. She was going to help Jacob play a cruel trick on his brother and father so that he would get the blessing instead.

She cooked Isaac's favorite dinner, put Esau's clothes on Jacob, then tied goatskin on to Jacob's arms to make them feel hairy.

Jacob went to his father with the soup. Isaac was tricked and thought it was Esau! So Isaac gave Jacob his special blessing.

Suddenly Esau came back from hunting with a tasty meal for his father.

"Who are you?" asked Isaac.

"Your son, Esau!" replied the hairy son.

"I have been tricked!" trembled Isaac. "Jacob has taken your blessing!"

Jacob ran away to live with his uncle Laban, as far away from angry Esau as he could go!

SPOT the DIFFERENCES

There are six differences between these two pictures. Circle each one as you find it.

NAME the BROTHER

Unscramble these letters to find the name of Esau's twin brother.

JOBAC

J A C O B

ESAU'S MAZE

Draw a line between Esau and the tent without crossing any of the red lines.

Joseph's Special Coat

Genesis 37:1–11

Jacob got married and had many children: twelve sons and one daughter. Jacob also had a very large flock of sheep and goats.

Jacob loved all his children, but one was his favorite: Joseph. Jacob loved him more than any of the others. This made Joseph feel pleased, but it made the other brothers feel very jealous indeed!

One day, Jacob gave Joseph a fabulous coat to wear. "Where's *our* coat?" his brothers muttered. "Why does Dad love him more than us?" They grew very angry.

One night Joseph had a strange dream. He told his brothers all about it the next day. But they didn't like what they heard!

"I dreamed we were all in the fields, gathering corn. Suddenly your sheaves of corn all made a circle around my sheaf of corn and bowed down to it!"

"Do you think you will rule over us?" sniggered the brothers. They hated Joseph. They were fed up.

To make matters worse, Joseph had

another strange dream. Again, he told his brothers all about it:

"I dreamed I saw the sun and moon and eleven stars, all bowing down to me!"

"Not again!" said his brothers. "Who does he think he is?! Does he think that his whole family will bow down to him now?"

The brothers were so angry they wanted to get rid of Joseph. They waited for the right moment. . . .

COLOR the COAT

Use crayons or markers to make Joseph's coat beautiful.

COUNTING PUZZLE

1. How many of Joseph's brothers can you see?

2. How many of Joseph's brothers have sticks?

3. How many sheep can you count in the picture?

4. How many goats can you count in the picture?

A Slave in Egypt

Genesis 37:12–36; 39:1—46:30

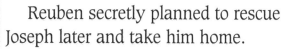

Joseph's brothers had a plan to get rid of their brother once and for all. They were filled with resentment.

One day, when they were looking after the sheep in the fields, Joseph came up to them.

Joseph's brothers had seen him coming. "Here comes the dreamer!" they laughed. "Let's kill him and throw him into a dry well. We'll tell Dad that a wild animal killed him. He'll never know."

But Reuben liked Joseph.

"No, let's not kill him," said Reuben. "Let's just throw him in the well."

Reuben secretly planned to rescue Joseph later and take him home.

Joseph arrived in the fields.

"How's it going?" asked Joseph.

Suddenly, the brothers grabbed Joseph, ripped off his fine coat, and threw him into the well.

"Help!" shouted Joseph. "What are you doing to me?!"

The brothers did not explain. They sat down to eat their lunch. Then some of the brothers saw a group of traders on their way to Egypt with camels. "Let's sell him to the traders!" said the brothers.

So Joseph was sold to be a slave and taken to Egypt.

The brothers were given twenty pieces of silver in return. They killed a goat and dipped Joseph's torn coat in the blood. They went to their father, Jacob, and told him the bad news. They didn't tell him the truth.

"A wild animal has killed Joseph!" wailed Jacob. "My son is dead!"

Meanwhile, Joseph was sold to a man named Potiphar, one of the king's officers.

Many years later, the brothers went to Egypt looking for food. They didn't expect to see Joseph again. But Joseph had done well for himself in Egypt. He was now in favor with the king and had a gold chain around his neck!

Joseph tested his brothers and knew that they were sorry for what they had done to him all those years ago. Joseph forgave them, hugged them, and was reunited with his father. Jacob was overjoyed to find his son alive again.

COLORED BAGS

This camel is carrying a heavy load of bags. How many of each color is he carrying?

ODD BIRD OUT

Check the birds that cannot fly.

FIND the BIRDS

These seven birds above are hidden in the picture below.
Can you find and circle them?

A Baby in a Basket

Exodus 2:1–10

Many years had passed since Joseph lived in Egypt. There was a new cruel king on the throne. He turned the Israelite people into his slaves. He made them work all day in the baking sun.

The king was afraid the slaves might turn against him, so he commanded his soldiers to drown the newborn boys of each Israelite family in the River Nile!

One mother hid her baby for three months where the soldiers could not find him. When the baby

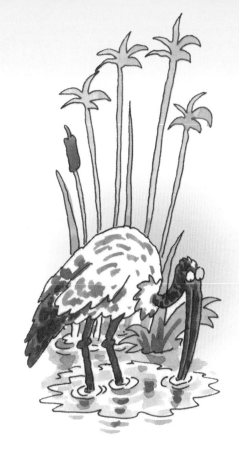

started to grow too big for the hiding place, she made a special basket of reeds, painted it with tar to make it waterproof, and put her baby in it. Lovingly she carried the basket down to the river and hid it in the reeds while the baby's sister, Miriam, watched from a distance.

When the king's daughter came down to the river to bathe, the princess heard the baby crying.

"An Israelite baby!" she cried.

Miriam stepped forward bravely. "Shall I find someone to feed him?"

When the princess agreed, Miriam ran to fetch her own mother.

"Look after the baby for me until he is big enough to live in the palace," said the princess. "I will pay you."

The baby was named Moses. He grew big and strong and lived in the royal palace.

CONNECT the PAIRS

There are two of each of these things in the picture.
Draw a line between the pairs.

frog

beetle

duck

fish

dragonfly

CATCH a FISH

This ibis bird is trying to catch fish to eat.
Draw over the line that goes to the fish.

A

B

C

D

Let My People Go

Exodus 3:1—12:51

"Moses! Moses!" came God's voice. "I have seen how cruel the ruler of Egypt is to my people. I have heard the slaves crying. I will bring them out of Egypt and take them to a land of their own. Go to the king of Egypt. Tell him to let my people go!"

Moses was astonished.

"But I am nobody special!" said Moses. "Why should the king listen to me?"

"I will be with you," said God. "Now go!"

So Moses and his brother Aaron went to the king of Egypt.

"The Lord, the God of Israel, says you must let His people go!" said Moses.

The king of Egypt laughed.

"No, I will not let my slaves go!"

"Then disasters will strike Egypt," said Moses.

Moses went down to the River Nile and put his stick in the water. The water turned to blood. All the fish died. But the king refused to listen to Moses.

God sent a plague of frogs. They hopped into the houses and into the kitchens. Then came a gigantic swarm of gnats and then flies to bite the Egyptians.

Next came a terrible disease that killed the animals in the fields. Horses, donkeys, cows, sheep, and goats lay dead on the ground.

People found terrible boils on their skin.

Hailstones pelted the land. Locusts ate all the crops. But still the king would not listen to Moses.

So God sent darkness to cover the land. Then every firstborn son of Egypt died. The king of Egypt sent for Moses. "Get out of my land!" he wailed. "And take your people. I will let them go."

Moses led the Israelite people out of Egypt.

ADDING UP

Add up the number of frogs in
each of these sums and write the
answer in the box.

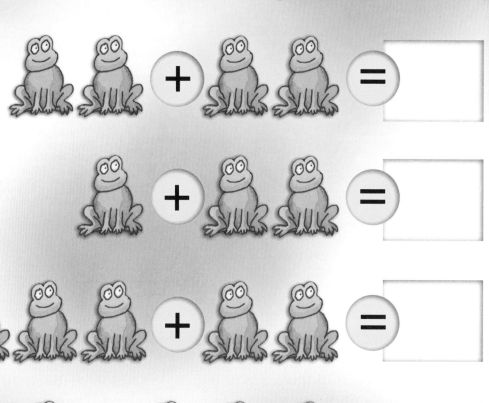

How many frogs are there all together?

ODD ONE OUT

Three of these pictures of Moses are the same, but one is different. Write the number of the one that is different here.

The Great Escape

Exodus 13:17—15:21

God led His people out of Egypt through the desert and toward the Red Sea. During the day God went in front of them in a pillar of cloud to show the way. During the night, God went in front of them in a pillar of fire to give them light.

They camped near the Red Sea.

But it wasn't long before the king of Egypt changed his mind.

"What have I done?!" he shouted. "Now I have lost all my slaves! I must get those people back here to work for me!"

So the king sent his soldiers after the Israelites!

He got his war chariot ready and his army. There were six hundred of the finest chariots in Egypt, horses and drivers and many more soldiers besides.

The Israelites were trapped by the Red Sea.

"What can we do now?" they wailed to Moses. "If we turn back, we will be captured by the king. If we go forward, we will surely drown in the Red Sea! Moses, why did you bring us here to die? Why didn't you leave us alone where we were? It is better to be a slave than to die in the desert!"

"Don't be afraid!" replied Moses. "You will see what God will do to save you today. The Lord will fight for you."

God had a plan. He told Moses to lift his stick and hold it over the waters of the sea. The water divided, and the Israelites were able to walk across on the dry land!

As soon as the people had crossed the Red Sea, Moses held out his stick again. God sent a powerful wind to close up the waters of the sea. All the Egyptians who had been chasing Moses and his people were washed away by the sea and drowned.

Moses and the Israelites sang a song of praise to God for rescuing them from the evil king of Egypt. They were on a journey to the promised land.

STRANGE SHEEP

Can you see what is wrong with each of these pictures? Circle the mistakes.

COMPLETE the PICTURE

Can you find where these puzzle pieces fit in the main picture? Write the number of the pieces next to the spaces where they fit.

Ten Commandments

Exodus 20:1–7

God's people were now free from slavery, but as they traveled through the desert, they became hot and thirsty, tired and grumpy. God helped Moses find water that poured from a rock. God provided quail for the people to eat and sweet manna that they collected each morning.

When they reached Mount Sinai, Moses left the people while he climbed up to meet with God, hidden by thick clouds. When Moses returned, he had two large pieces of stone. God had given him rules to help the people live happily together.

"God is the only God. Love him alone."

"Don't make idols or worship anything else but God."

"Respect God's name. It is special and holy."

"Keep the Sabbath as a special day."

"Love and respect your parents."

"Don't murder anyone."

"Don't steal someone else's wife or husband."

"Do not steal anything from anyone."

"Do not lie to anyone."

"Don't be jealous of other people's things."

These became known as the ten commandments.

GET to the MOUNTAIN

Start here. Help Moses get to the mountain.

58

A SPECIAL MOUNTAIN

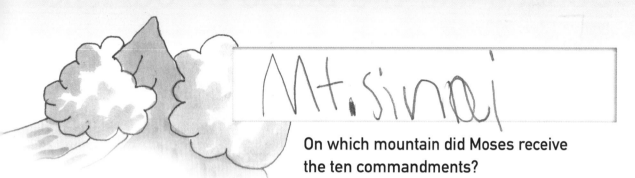

Mt. sinai

On which mountain did Moses receive the ten commandments?

IN the CROWD

Draw a line connecting each of these people to where they are in the crowd below.

Joshua and the Battle of Jericho

Joshua 1:1–6; 5:13—6:20

Joshua was chosen by God to be the next leader of His people.

"I will be with you, as I was with Moses," said God. "I will never leave you. Don't be afraid, for I, the Lord, am with you wherever you go."

The Israelite people were still on their way to the promised land.

First the people had to pass through the city of Jericho. The stone walls of the city were very thick and impossible to get through. The gates were locked, so the Israelites could not get into the city. Guards kept watch day and night.

Joshua believed God would help them. He listened to God's plan.

God told Joshua to choose seven priests who would carry trumpets made of rams' horns. They were to lead the army in a march around the city once every day for six days, blowing their trumpets.

On the seventh day, the priests would march around the city six times. On the seventh time, the priests would sound a long, loud note on their rams' horns, and the people would give a great shout.

So that is exactly what Joshua and the people did. They marched around the city each day until, on the seventh day and on the seventh march, the people gave a great shout.

The walls of the city collapsed!

Joshua and his people captured the city. Joshua always listened to God's words and was careful to obey God's laws.

When Joshua was a very old man, he told the Israelites to keep on serving God.

"As for me and my family," said Joshua, "we will always serve the Lord."

HOW MANY PRIESTS?

1. How many have pink belts?

2. How many have yellow belts?

3. How many have blue belts?

MAZE

Help the priest find his way into Jericho.

Samuel's Sleepless Night

1 Samuel 3:1–21

Hannah had longed for a child for many years. She prayed for a child of her own. God heard her prayers and blessed her with a son. She called him Samuel.

Hannah wanted Samuel to serve God in the temple at Shiloh as a way of thanking Him for her son. So Samuel lived far away from his parents' home.

Samuel helped Eli the priest, who was a very old man. Eli loved God and served Him. But his sons did not follow God's laws.

One night, when Eli was asleep, Samuel heard a voice calling his name.

"Samuel! Samuel!"

"Yes, here I am," said Samuel, running into Eli's room. He thought it was Eli who had called him.

"I did not call you. Go back to bed, Samuel," said Eli. So Samuel went back to bed. The voice called again: "Samuel! Samuel!"

Again, Samuel ran to Eli. "Here I am!" he said.

"I didn't call," said Eli. "Go back to bed, Samuel!" Again Samuel settled back down in his bed. But not for long.

"Samuel! Samuel!" came the voice. He ran to Eli.

This time, Eli realized who was calling. It was the voice of God.

"If He calls again, say, 'Speak, Lord, Your servant is listening.'"

So Samuel went back to bed. This time he was ready.

"Samuel! Samuel!" came the voice.

"Speak, Lord, your servant is listening," said Samuel.

And God spoke to Samuel. In the morning, Samuel told Eli all that God had said. God was going to punish Eli's sons for the bad things they were doing.

Everything He said came true.

SPOT the DIFFERENCES

Find eight differences
between the two pictures
and circle them.

DOT-to-DOT

Connect the dots from 1 to 23 to find something that helped Samuel see at night.

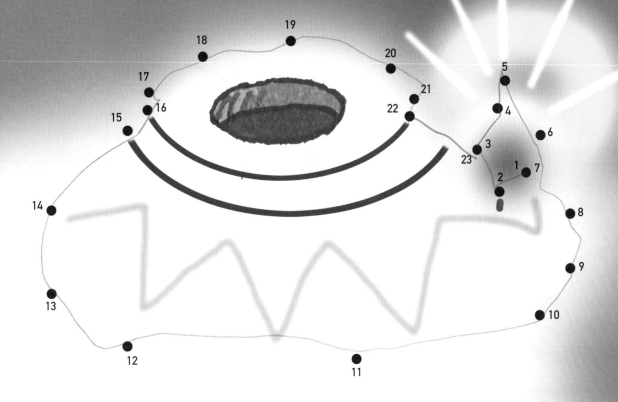

What is it?

Candel

The Shepherd Boy

1 Samuel 16:1–23

David was a handsome young man. He took care of his father Jesse's sheep and could scare away wild animals that came near. He could play the harp and sing very well.

The prophet Samuel was sent by God to choose one of Jesse's sons to be the next king. Samuel was worried and asked God, "What if the present king, Saul, hears about this! He will be very angry and might even kill me!"

But God told Samuel to go visit Jesse's family.

One of Jesse's sons was very tall and handsome, but this was not the man God wanted to be king. Jesse brought seven of his sons to Samuel, but none of them was the one God had chosen.

Samuel asked, "Have you any more sons?"

"Only the youngest," replied Jesse. "He is out looking after the sheep."

Jesse sent for David to come and see Samuel. God said to Samuel, "This is the one. Anoint him!"

So Samuel took some olive oil and anointed David in front of all the brothers. From that day on, God's spirit was with David.

The present king was named Saul. He was a troubled man. He didn't always do as God wanted. He was often moody and depressed.

"I need someone to play the harp for me!" said King Saul.

One of the king's servants told Saul about David. "David is brave and handsome, and he plays the harp well."

"Bring him to me," said King Saul.

So David came to play his harp for Saul. Whenever the king was depressed, David played beautiful music and Saul felt much better again.

King Saul didn't know that David had been anointed to be the next king of Israel.

69

FIND the PAIR

Which two of these pictures of David are exactly the same?

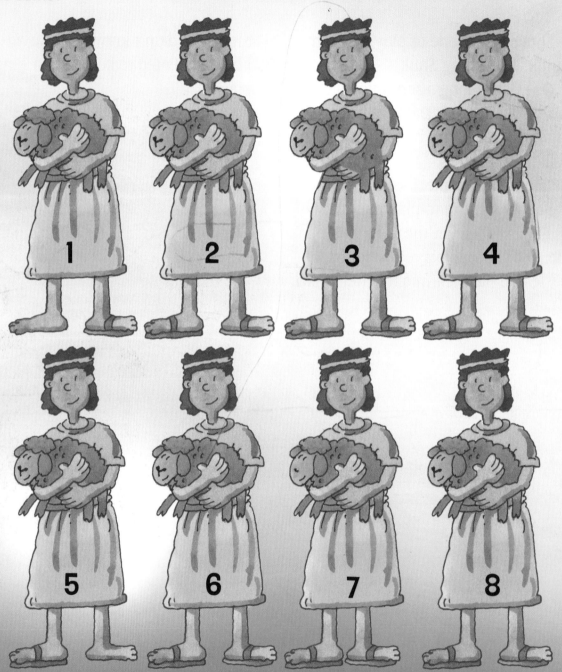

COMPLETE the PICTURE

Color in the hats, hands, headdresses, and beards in the picture below.

David and the Giant

1 Samuel 17:1–50

King Saul's army was fighting the Philistines. It was always fighting the Philistines! Three of David's brothers were in the army.

One day, their father sent David to the army camp with some food to give to his brothers.

As he came near to the army camp, David heard a booming voice. It came from a giant of a man! It was Goliath, the Philistine champion.

King Saul had promised a big reward to the man who could kill Goliath. But no one dared to try!

"No one should be afraid of this man! He is not just challenging us. He is challenging God himself!" said David. "I will fight him! God has saved me from the lion and the bear when I have been looking after my sheep. God will save me now."

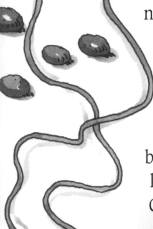

David tried on the king's armor, but it was far too big. He decided to meet the giant without it. David went to the brook with his sling, picked up five smooth stones, and put them in his bag.

When Goliath saw David, he laughed a cruel laugh.

"You have a sword and a spear," said David, "but I have God on my side!"

David took a stone out of his bag, put it in his sling, whizzed it around his head, and fired it at the giant. The stone hit Goliath in the middle of his forehead, and he fell to the ground with a mighty crash!

David grabbed Goliath's sword and chopped off his head.

When the Philistines saw that their hero was dead, they ran away as fast as they could! God had given David the victory. All the people cheered for him.

FIND the WORDS

Can you find these six words hidden in the grid? Draw a circle around each word.

spear

stone

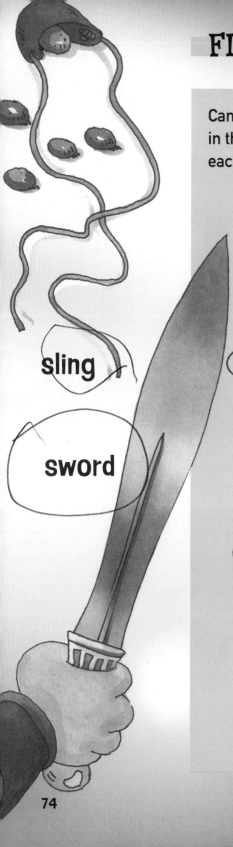

sling

sword

a	t	s	l	i	n	g
e	a	t	a	e	d	o
s	w	o	r	d	a	r
s	e	n	r	r	v	s
s	p	e	a	r	i	d
s	l	i	r	x	d	g
g	o	l	i	a	t	h

Goliath

David

COUNT the SPEARS

1. How many of the soldiers in the picture are carrying spears?

2. How many of the soldiers in the picture have no spear?

3. How many of the soldiers in the picture are wearing something on their heads?

2

4. How many soldiers are there in the picture?

God Looks After Elijah

1 Kings 17:1–16

Elijah had been called by God to be a prophet. He gave messages from God to the people of Israel and their king.

One day Elijah went to see King Ahab, who did not care about following God's ways. Ahab's wife was even worse. She worshipped the false god Baal.

Elijah warned the king to listen to God, but Ahab and his wife refused to listen.

"Then I must tell you this," said Elijah. "There will be no rain for the next two or three years until God sends it!"

Now Elijah's life was in danger. God told him to go east and hide near the brook in the Kerith Ravine.

God looked after Elijah. He ordered ravens to bring him bread and meat every morning and every evening. And Elijah drank the water in the brook of the ravine until it dried up.

Then God told Elijah to go to a town called Zarephath, where a widow would help him.

Elijah saw the woman gathering firewood. "Please bring me a drink of water," Elijah said to her. "And some bread, too, please."

The widow and her son were nearly starving, as all her food was running out. During the drought there was no rain to water the crops. But she kindly offered to make a small loaf of bread for Elijah with the little bit of flour and oil she had left.

"Don't worry," said Elijah. "You won't starve. God says the jar of flour and this jug of oil will never be empty until the day it rains again," said Elijah.

Sure enough, there was always enough flour and oil in the jar to feed them all! God looked after Elijah.

BIG and SMALL

Put a **B** next to the biggest raven and an **S** by the smallest.

FIND and COUNT

Find and count these things in the big picture, and write how many there are in the boxes.

plates — 4

cups — 2

chunks of bread — 1

full bowls — 1

trees — 3

Fire from Heaven

1 Kings 18:16–45

It was nearly three years since Elijah had seen King Ahab. The land was dry and parched. Now God told Elijah to return to see the king again.

Elijah was not afraid. He gave the king God's message as he had done before.

"You have turned away from the true God and worshipped Baal instead. Now we will have a contest to see who is the one true God. The people must choose whom they will worship. Ask the prophets of Baal to come to Mount Carmel."

When the hundreds of prophets who worshipped Baal had gathered on the mountain, Elijah spoke to them all.

"The prophets of Baal will put one bull on their altar. I will put another bull on the altar of the Lord. The Baal worshippers will call on Baal to roast their bull. I will call on the one true God to roast the other bull. We will see who answers!"

The prophets of Baal shouted all day, but no fire came.

"Shout louder!" said Elijah. "Maybe

80

he is daydreaming, or on the toilet! Or maybe he has gone on a journey! He might be asleep, and you'll have to wake him up!"

There was still no answer from Baal.

Next it was Elijah's turn. Elijah asked his servants to pour water on the altar three times. It ran down the altar and filled a trench around the altar.

Elijah prayed loudly, "Answer my prayer, O God. Show these people that You are the true God of Israel! Show these people that You are God and that You are bringing them back to Yourself!"

God answered Elijah's prayer. He sent down fire from heaven. It burnt up the bull, the wood, and the stones and dried up all the water in the trench!

The people watching were amazed and shouted, "The Lord is God!"

The prophets of Baal tried to run away, but Elijah did not let them escape.

Then clouds began to appear in the sky. The drought was ended. God was sending rain again to water the land.

MATCH the PICTURE

Only one of these prophets is exactly like the one in the box.
Put a check (✔) next to him.

COLORS

Trace the word for each answer.

Elijah's robe is:

Elijah's headdress is:

The prophets' hats are:

The flames are:

red

green

blue

red and yellow

83

Naaman and the Little Servant Girl

2 Kings 5:1–15

Naaman had won many battles and was a very important general in the Syrian army. One day, Naaman's army took a little girl from Israel to be a servant in Naaman's household. The girl worked hard and liked her master and mistress.

Naaman fell ill with a terrible disease. It was leprosy. His skin turned white and sore, and no one could cure him.

The little girl in Naaman's household said to her mistress one day, "I wish that my master would go and see Elisha, the prophet in Samaria! I am sure he could heal Naaman of this disease!"

Naaman had nothing to lose. He got permission to go and took a letter and gifts to King Joram.

The king was horrified when Naaman arrived in Samaria with his horses and chariots. He didn't know how he could help the commander. But Elisha told the king to send Naaman to him so that he could show him that there was a God in Israel who could heal people.

When Naaman arrived at the prophet's house, he expected to be welcomed in. But Elisha would not see Naaman. Instead he just sent a message to him.

"Go and wash seven times in the River Jordan. Then you will be healed!"

Naaman was angry. He thought Elisha would at least come out and pray for him.

"Just try it and see," said Naaman's servants. "If he had asked you to do something difficult, you would have done it!"

So Naaman went down to the river and dipped himself in it seven times. To his amazement, he was completely healed. His white, wrinkled skin became as soft and pink as a baby's skin!

Naaman returned to Elisha and said, "Now I know that there is no other god but the God of Israel."

Naaman returned home, amazed at what God had done for him.

FIND the DUCKS

How many ducks can you see in the picture? Draw a circle around each of them, and write the number in the box.

MAZE

Help Naaman find his way to the Jordan River.

Daniel in the Lions' Den

Daniel 6:1–24

Daniel loved God and wanted to serve Him wherever he went.

One day, Daniel was taken captive by a foreign king and made to serve in the king's court. Daniel was certain that he would always serve God, even if it got him into trouble.

Daniel worked hard and became an important leader in the king's court. But some men were very jealous of him. They tried to get him into trouble.

The king had made a rule that, for thirty days, everyone in the land must worship no one but the king. Anyone found worshipping someone else must be thrown to the lions!

Of course, Daniel continued to worship God. So the jealous men arrested Daniel and took him to be fed to the hungry lions!

The king was very upset. He felt he had been tricked into making the rule about worshipping only the king. But now there was no choice. He had to let Daniel be thrown to the lions.

"May your God rescue you!" said the king.

It was a long night for the king. He waited to see what had happened to Daniel. He feared the worst.

At last, morning came, and the king ran to the lions' den.

"Daniel! Are you alive?" he called. He didn't expect to hear a reply.

"Yes, I'm alive!" shouted Daniel. "God sent an angel to shut the mouths of the lions. They did not hurt me."

The king was very happy to see Daniel again. He was angry with the jealous men in his court and ordered that they be thrown to the lions instead!

Now Daniel was free so he could pray to God wherever he liked. And the king knew that Daniel's God was the true and living God who had power to save.

COLOR the DOTS

Color in all the shapes marked with a dot to find out what is hiding in the cave.

Write the answer
in the box.

COUNT the LIONS

How many times can you find the word *lion* in the grid?

6

x	l	a	w	v	l
l	i	o	n	a	i
m	o	p	l	w	o
r	n	l	i	o	n
v	p	s	o	t	a
l	i	o	n	x	w

Jonah Runs Away

Jonah 1:1—3:10

"Go to Nineveh!" God said to Jonah. "Speak to the people and tell them I know all the terrible things they are doing. Tell them they must stop! They must do good things and learn to be kind to each other—or I must destroy them!"

But Jonah ran away. He did not want to go to Nineveh and do as God asked. He was afraid. He ran in the opposite direction and boarded a ship with a crew ready to sail to Spain.

Jonah felt safe. He went below deck, settled down, and fell asleep. He did not notice the storm that was brewing or the waves lashing the ship. Jonah slept on.

God made the storm rock the ship violently. All the sailors feared for their lives. They threw their cargo overboard, but still the storm raged on.

Then the sailors found that Jonah was sleeping. They woke him up and made him call on God.

"It's all my fault!" Jonah shouted above the roaring wind. "I ran away from God. You must throw me into the sea, and then you will be safe!"

The sailors did not want to harm Jonah, but they realized there was nothing else they could do. They threw him overboard, and at once the sea became calm.

The ship sailed away, leaving the sailors amazed at God's power.

Jonah sank down into the deep, cold, dark sea. He thought he would drown and called to God to help him.

God answered Jonah's prayer. A huge fish opened his mouth and swallowed Jonah. There Jonah prayed to God and sang praises to Him.

After three days, the fish spat Jonah out on a beach.

God asked Jonah again to go to Nineveh. This time Jonah obeyed.

Jonah told the people of Nineveh what God had said. They listened to God's message and were sorry when they realized all the wrong things they had done. They turned back to God and asked Him to forgive them.

God loved the people. He was no longer angry with them. They had listened, said they were sorry, and changed their ways. God was kind and forgave them.

COLOR the PICTURE

Color this picture of Jonah being thrown into the sea.

FIND the FISH

How many huge fish can you find in the sea?

5

Old Testament Puzzle Solutions

Page 10

The ten differences are circled on the picture.

Page 14

apple, cherries, banana

Page 15

4 blue flowers; 3 rabbits; 1 frog; 2 mice.

Page 18

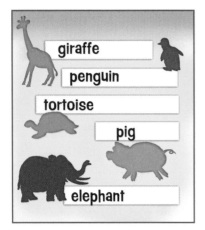

giraffe

penguin

tortoise

pig

elephant

Page 19

The words are circled in the grid.

a	g	h	p	w	v
l	i	o	n	x	a
f	m	r	p	i	g
o	a	s	m	d	a
x	p	e	o	w	l
d	o	g	v	w	m

Page 22

Page 23

5

Page 26

There are 11 sheep.

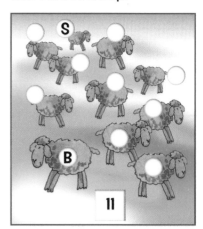

11

Page 30

The match is picture number 4.

In the picture: sheep, cattle, donkey.

Page 31

There are 12 stars.

The odd one out is circled on the picture.

Page 34

The jumbled name is **Jacob**.

Page 35

Page 39

1:10, 2:2, 3:7, 4:3.

Page 42

Yellow: 3 ; Red: 4; Blue: 3.

Page 43

The birds that cannot fly are 4 and 8.

Page 46

Page 47

Line B.

Page 50

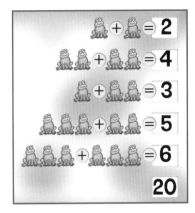

Page 51

The odd picture is number 4.

Page 54

Page 55

Page 58

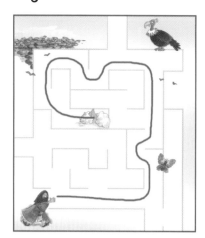

Page 59

Mount Sinai

Page 62

Pink: 5; Green 1, Blue: 2.

Page 63

Page 66

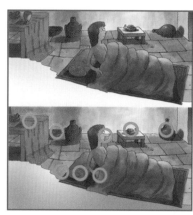

Page 67

A lamp

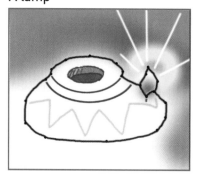

Page 70

Matching pair: 6 and 8.

Page 74

a	t	s	l	i	n	g
e	a	t	a	e	d	o
s	w	o	r	d	a	r
s	e	n	r	r	v	s
s	p	e	a	r	i	d
s	l	i	r	x	d	g
g	o	l	i	a	t	h

Page 75

13 soldiers are carrying spears.
1 soldier has no spear.
2 soldiers are wearing hats.
14 soldiers are in the picture.

Page 78

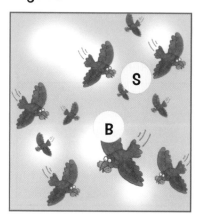

Page 79

Plates: 4; cups: 2; bread: 2; full bowls: 1; trees: 3.

Page 82

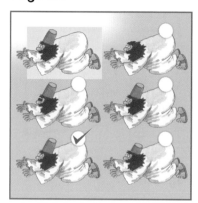

Page 83

Elijah's robe is:

Elijah's head dress is:

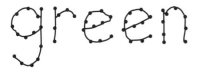

The prophets' hats are:

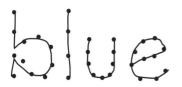

The flames are:

and

Page 86

Page 90

Page 91

There are 6 lions in the word search.

x	l	a	w	v	l
l	i	o	n	a	i
m	o	p	l	w	o
r	n	l	i	o	n
v	p	s	o	t	a
l	i	o	n	x	w

Page 95

There are 5 huge fish in the sea.

The New Testament

Mary's Baby

Luke 1:26–38; 2:1–7

God sent the angel Gabriel to a town called Nazareth. He brought news for a young woman named Mary.

"Mary, don't be afraid!" said the angel. "God has chosen you. You will have a baby boy, and you will call Him Jesus. He will be great. He will be the Son of God. His kingdom will last forever."

Mary was amazed. She didn't understand why God had chosen her. But she was happy to obey God.

"I am God's servant," she said. "Let it be as you have said."

Mary was soon going to marry Joseph, a carpenter in Nazareth.

The Roman emperor wanted to count all the people in the land. So Joseph had to go to his family's hometown of Bethlehem. Mary went too. It was a long way to travel, and

Mary's baby was soon to be born. Their donkey carried their bundles of clothes and supplies.

The road was dry and stony. Mary felt very hot and tired. She hoped they would soon reach their journey's end and have a good rest.

But when Mary and Joseph arrived in Bethlehem, there was no room for them except the place where the animals were kept.

There in Bethlehem, Mary's baby was born. She wrapped her little Son in strips of cloth. She laid Him in the soft hay in a manger. She gazed at the baby and remembered what the angel had told her. This was God's own Son. His kingdom would last forever.

Jesus had come into the world!

COMPLETE the PICTURES

All these creatures have something missing. Draw in the missing parts.

Draw the tail on the mouse.

Draw the horns on the ox.

a

b

c

FIND and COUNT

How many mice can you find in the picture below?

SOUNDS

Match the sound to the source. Write the number of the sound in the circles below.

1. squeek squeek

2. maaa maaa

3. waah waah

4. twit twoo

Draw horns on the goat.

d

The Angels and the Shepherds

Luke 2:8–20

On the hills near Bethlehem, shepherds were looking after their sheep. It was a clear night, and the shepherds looked up at the stars.

Suddenly, the sky was filled with a blinding light. An angel of the Lord appeared!

"Don't be afraid!" said the angel. "I bring good news and great joy to you! Tonight in Bethlehem your Savior has been born! He is Christ the Lord. This is how you will know it is Him—you will find the baby lying in a manger, wrapped in strips of cloth."

The sky was filled with angels praising God:

"Glory to God in the highest heaven, and on earth peace and goodwill to all!"

It was a glorious sight!

The shepherds knew what they must do. They left their sheep at once and hurried down into the town.

"We must see this king whom God has told us about!" they said.

They found Mary and Joseph and the baby lying in the manger. He was their Savior!

"It is all just as the angel said!" they exclaimed.

Mary heard how the angels had appeared to the shepherds, and she treasured their words in her heart.

The shepherds went back to their sheep, singing songs of praise to God, and telling everyone about the wonderful things they had seen.

WORD SEARCH

Draw a circle around the words the angel said
to the shepherds.

m	o	d	b	k	p
a	f	r	a	i	d
n	s	k	b	n	s
g	r	t	y	g	s
e	g	o	o	d	a
r	a	n	e	w	s

afraid   good   news   baby   king   manger

CONNECT the DOTS

Connect the dots to see what the man is carrying, and color in the picture.

HOW MANY GOATS?

How many goats can you count on this page?

The Journey of the Wise Men

Matthew 2:1–15

Wise men in an eastern country were studying the stars.

They had spotted a new star, shining brightly in the sky.

"It means a new king has been born!" they said. "We must travel west and find Him. We will take gifts to honor Him!"

The wise men set off across the desert, following the star.

The star seemed to have stopped over the city of Jerusalem. The wise men found the palace of King Herod and asked to see the new baby king.

But Herod knew nothing about a new king. The teachers of the Law looked in their scrolls. "It is written

here that a leader will come from Bethlehem!"

So the wise men set off again to Bethlehem. King Herod wanted them to return and tell him when they had found the new king. But Herod didn't want to honor the Child. He wanted to get rid of Him!

The wise men reached Bethlehem.

"Look! The star is shining over there!" they said, pointing to a poor house.

They went quietly into the house and found Mary with her little Son, Jesus.

The wise men knelt down before the boy and worshipped Him.

"We have found the new king!" they said.

They took out their gifts to give to Jesus: gold, frankincense, and myrrh.

Mary looked at the gifts in wonder and amazement.

When it was time to leave, God warned the wise men in a dream to go home by another road. Mary and Joseph took Jesus away from Bethlehem to safety in Egypt. The boy grew up there until King Herod had died and it was safe to return.

MAZE

Show the wise men the correct way to follow the star
and find Jesus.

SOMETHING'S WRONG

Find and circle six things that are wrong with this picture.

The Four Fishermen

Luke 5:1–11

Jesus grew up and began to talk to people about God.

One day, He was standing on the shore of Lake Gennesaret. He saw two fishing boats near the shore. The fishermen had pulled the boats on to the sandy beach and were washing their nets.

Jesus asked if He could stand in one of the boats and talk to the crowd of people who had come to listen to Him. People were pushing and jostling each other. They all wanted to listen to Jesus.

The boat Jesus picked out belonged to Peter and Andrew. They were happy to let Jesus stand in their boat.

When Jesus had finished speaking, He told Peter to push the boat out and let down the fishing nets.

"Master," said Peter, "we have fished all night but caught nothing. Not even a squid. But if you say so, we'll try again."

Peter let down the nets one more time. Suddenly the nets were filled with an enormous catch of fish! They slapped and slithered about in the net so hard that it nearly broke! Peter called to his friends, James and John, who were in the other boat, to come and help.

Peter was amazed and fell at Jesus' feet.

"Don't be afraid," said Jesus. "Follow Me!"

So Peter, Andrew, James, and John left their nets and followed Jesus. They were His first disciples.

SHAPES

In the picture below...

1. Which shapes are round?

2. Which shapes are square?

3. Which shapes are triangles?

COMPLETE the PICTURE

Each of these details belong in the big picture. Write the number of the detail into the space it came from.

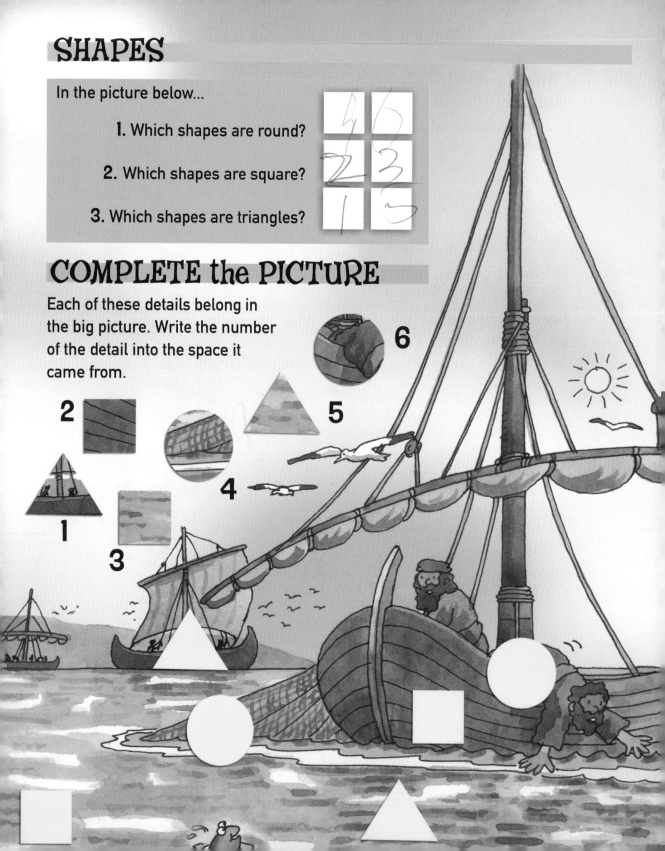

COUNT the COLORS

Count the number of fish of each
color in the net.

1. How many
    red fish?

2. How many
    yellow fish?

3. How many
    blue fish?

4. How many fish
    altogether?

Jesus Meets Matthew

Matthew 9:9–13

Everyone hated tax collectors. They often took more money than they needed and kept the extra money for themselves. They made themselves richer while ordinary people became poorer.

Matthew was collecting taxes when he first met Jesus.

"Come, follow Me!" invited Jesus. Matthew did not need to be asked twice. Without looking back, he left his booth and joined the growing number of men whom Jesus had called to be His friends and disciples.

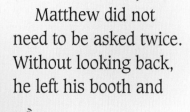

Many of these men were fishermen. Matthew did not really fit in. But he knew that he belonged where Jesus was.

Then Matthew held a great feast in his house and invited Jesus. There was wonderful food and wine. It was a huge celebration. Matthew invited many different guests, including tax collectors.

Teachers of the Law grumbled about this, asking, "Why do Jesus and

His friends eat and drink with the tax collectors? No one likes them!"

Jesus heard what they were saying and answered, "Healthy people do not need a doctor. These people need My help."

Matthew became a special disciple of Jesus and followed Him wherever He went. His whole life was going to change forever.

Matthew had spent his life counting money and taxes. Now he would follow Jesus and leave his old life behind.

FIND the MISTAKES

Circle the eight things that are wrong with this picture.

HOW MUCH?

Tax collectors counted money.
Add up the coins in each of these sums.

IN the BAG

How many coins are there in the bag?

The Four Kind Friends

Luke 5:17–26

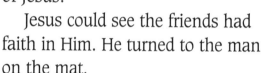

Jesus was inside a house, talking to teachers of the Law. The room was very crowded, and no one else could squeeze inside.

Suddenly four men arrived at the house, carrying another on a mat between them. The man on the mat could not walk. He couldn't even sit up. He desperately needed help—and the four friends believed that Jesus could give it.

But the friends could not get through the crowd to Jesus.

"Let's try the roof!" said one of them.

They had made their way to where Jesus was. They were sure that if they could get to Jesus, Jesus would heal their friend.

So the men began to scrape away at the mud between the branches that made up the flat roof. Bits of dirt and twigs fell down on the people in the room below. Soon everyone stopped talking in the room and watched as the hole grew from a tiny one to a large gap big enough to lower the man and his mat down in front of Jesus!

Jesus could see the friends had faith in Him. He turned to the man on the mat.

"My son, your sins are forgiven."

"What is He saying?" muttered the teachers of the Law. "How can He forgive sins? Only God can do that!"

Jesus knew what they were saying and turned to them. "I will show you that the Son of Man can forgive sins."

Jesus turned to the man on the mat and said, "Pick up your mat and walk! Go home now."

Everyone watched in amazement as the man got up off the floor, rolled up his mat, and walked out of the house!

WHICH ROPE?

Only one of these ropes is still joined to the lame man's mat. Which one is it?

SPOT the DIFFERENCES

Can you circle seven differences between these two pictures?

The Disciples Learn from Jesus

Luke 6:12–16, 27–42

People crowded around Jesus wherever He went. They knew He could heal them, and they came to Him to ask for His help. As He touched them, they were healed. They also wanted to listen as Jesus told them that God loved them.

Jesus now had twelve friends who were His disciples: Peter and Andrew, James and John, Matthew, Philip, Bartholomew, Thomas, another James, Simon, Jude, and Judas Iscariot. Jesus taught His disciples many things they had not understood

before about how God wanted them to live.

"Love your enemies! Be kind to people who hurt you, and pray for them. Be generous to people who ask for your help. Do for other people the things you would like them to do for you."

"Don't criticize and judge other people, but ask for help to remove your own faults. Be forgiving as you wish to be forgiven yourselves."

TRUE or FALSE

Put a check next to those statements that are true, and put an X next to those that are false.

1. Jesus had eleven disciples.

2. Jesus had a disciple whose name was Brian.

3. Jesus told the crowd to judge their enemies.

4. Jesus told the crowd to be kind to those who hurt them.

DRAW a BOAT

Draw a small boat on the lake.

PUT the PICTURE BACK TOGETHER

Number these picture slices in the right order so that when arranged 1 to 5 the proper picture is formed.

The Story of the Two Houses

Luke 6:46–49

Jesus told many stories to the crowds who followed Him. Sometimes you could almost imagine the story in pictures.

One day He told this story:

"If you listen to My words and obey them, you will be like a wise man who built his house upon a rock.

"It took a long time for the man to build his house. He had to dig down deep to make strong foundations. He used strong stone to build the walls of the house. He sweated and worked very hard. At last it was finished. The man moved in and felt safe.

"In the winter, the weather turned bad! The rain poured down, strong winds blew, the rivers flooded, and many houses were washed away. But the house on the rock stood firm. Its foundations were strong and deep. The man was happy and knew that it was worth all that hard work.

"But if you don't listen to My words, you are like a foolish man who built his house on the shifting sand.

"'I don't think I can be bothered to make this house very strong!' said the man. 'I want to move in quickly. I don't think it will matter too much if the foundations are a bit near the surface. I just want to get the house ready before the winter.'

"He was a lazy man. But his house was soon ready, and the man moved in.

"But when winter came, so did the bad weather! The rain came down, the wind blew hard, the rivers flooded. The foolish man noticed cracks in his walls. The cracks grew bigger and bigger and bigger, then CRASH! The house came tumbling down and was washed away by the rains!"

MAZE

Help the wise man and the foolish man find the way to their own houses.

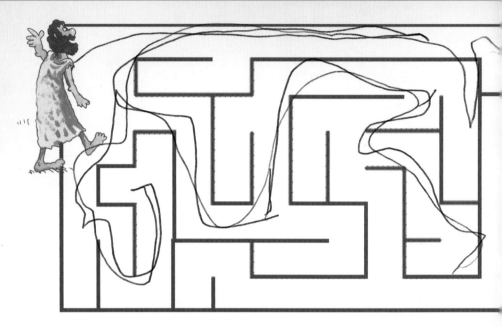

COLOR the PICTURE

Complete the picture by coloring it in.

The Big Storm

Mark 4:35–41

One day, Jesus got into a boat with His friends. It had been a tiring day.

"Let's go over to the other side of Lake Galilee," said Jesus.

Many of Jesus' disciples were fishermen. They knew about boats. Very soon, the water lapping against the side of the boat sent Jesus to sleep.

After they had been sailing for a little while, the wind changed, and some black clouds moved quickly across the sky. Soon a mighty storm was blowing. The boat was rocked about and began to fill with water!

Jesus was still fast asleep. His head was on a pillow. He didn't seem to notice the storm and the rocking boat at all!

"Wake up! Wake up!" the disciples called to Jesus. They had started to panic. "We are all going to drown!"

Jesus woke up. He stood up on the deck. He spoke to the winds and

commanded them to stop blowing. He spoke to the waves and ordered them to be calm.

All at once the storm vanished. The lake was completely calm again.

Then Jesus turned to His disciples and said, "Why were you so afraid? Don't you trust Me?"

The disciples were amazed. They looked at one another and said, "Who can this man be? Even the winds and waves obey Him!"

WHO'S THERE?

Which of these people sailed in the boat? Put
a check next to them.

WORD SEARCH

Find the words about storms in the grid.

storm   wind   ~~calm~~
rain   ~~wave~~   ~~water~~

Which word means the opposite of a storm? Mark it on the grid in red.

s	t	o	r	m	v
m	o	c	a	l	m
r	s	w	i	n	d
a	w	a	v	e	s
i	w	a	t	e	r
n	c	k	a	m	s

Dinner at Simon's House

Luke 7:36–48

Simon, one of the religious leaders, invited Jesus to have dinner with him. While they were eating, a woman came into the room, silently weeping. She knelt behind Jesus and washed His feet with her tears and wiped them with her long hair. She kissed His feet and bathed them in expensive perfume that she had brought in a jar.

Simon knew the woman was talked about in the city. She was not

respectable at all. Simon would have avoided her if he had met her in the street. But Jesus knew all about the woman, and He knew what Simon was thinking.

"Listen, Simon, I have a story to tell you," said Jesus. "A man loaned 500 pieces of silver to one man and 50 pieces to the other. Neither could repay him, so he kindly forgave them both so they didn't need to repay their debts to him. Who do you think loved him more afterward?"

Simon answered, "I suppose the one who owed him the most money."

"That's right," Jesus said. "A person who is forgiven little shows only a little love. But this woman has done many things of which she is ashamed. She has much to be forgiven, and she loves very much. "

Then Jesus said to the woman, "Your sins are forgiven."

HOW MANY?

How many of these things might
you be able to eat?
Put a check beside each one.

How many of these things
might you be able to eat?
Put an X beside each one.

140

WHAT CAN YOU SEE?

Check the five things that can be found in the picture below.

The Girl Who Came Back to Life

Luke 8:40–42, 49–56

Crowds of people followed Jesus wherever He went. A man called Jairus called out from the crowd:

"Jesus! Please help me! My only daughter is dying! We need Your help!"

As Jesus made His way to Jairus's house, He stopped to heal a woman who had been ill for many years. The crowds were pressing all around Jesus, and He couldn't get through very quickly.

Just then, a messenger came from Jairus's household to say, "It's too late. The girl has already died."

But Jesus said to Jairus, "Don't be afraid. Believe in Me, and she will be well."

When Jesus arrived at Jairus's house, everyone was crying and wailing loudly. It was a terrible sight.

"Don't worry," said Jesus kindly, "she is not dead. She is just sleeping."

He went into the house with Peter, John, and James and spoke to the girl.

"Get up, My child," He said gently. At once, life returned to her body, and she sat up! It was a miracle.

Jesus told her parents to give the girl something to eat and look after her.

They couldn't believe their eyes but were overjoyed to see their twelve-year-old daughter alive again.

They thanked Jesus with all their hearts.

LEFT or RIGHT?

Write **R** in the circle next to the right hands and **L** in the circle next to the left hands.

IT'S a PUZZLE

Show where the puzzle pieces go by writing the correct letter in each circle.

The Big Picnic

Matthew 14:13–21

Jesus and His disciples had been busy all day. People everywhere wanted to see Jesus. They had heard how He could make sick people well again, so they brought with them their old and unwell relatives. They wanted to hear what He said about God's kingdom. They wanted to know how much God loved them.

Now the sun was beginning to set, and there were still great crowds of people all around. They were in no hurry to go home.

"We must send the people off to get food in the villages," said the disciples. "They are hungry."

But Jesus replied, "They can eat here. We must give them some food."

"But there are thousands of people here!" said one of them. "No one could possibly afford to feed them all!"

"There is a young boy here with his packed lunch," said another. "But all he has is five pieces of bread and two fish," said Andrew. "That will never be enough to feed all these people."

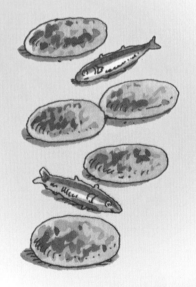

Jesus smiled and took the bread and fishes. He told the disciples to make the people sit in groups of about fifty people.

Then Jesus gave thanks to God for the food and broke it into pieces. He gave them to the disciples to share out among the crowd.

Everyone passed the food to another and shared it between them. Everyone ate and had more than enough. It was a great feast.

At the end, the disciples gathered up enough leftovers to fill twelve baskets.

"I am the bread of life," said Jesus later. "Whoever comes to Me will never be hungry; whoever believes in Me will never be thirsty."

WHICH ONE?

1. How many pieces of bread are there below?

2. How many fish can you see here?

3. Which is the odd fish out?

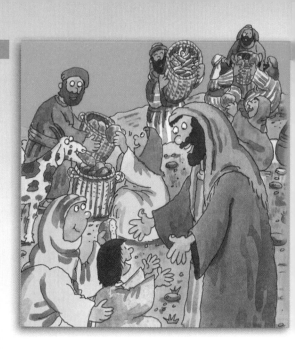

5. Put an **X** next to the smallest piece of bread and the smallest fish.

4. Put a check next to the biggest piece of bread and the biggest fish.

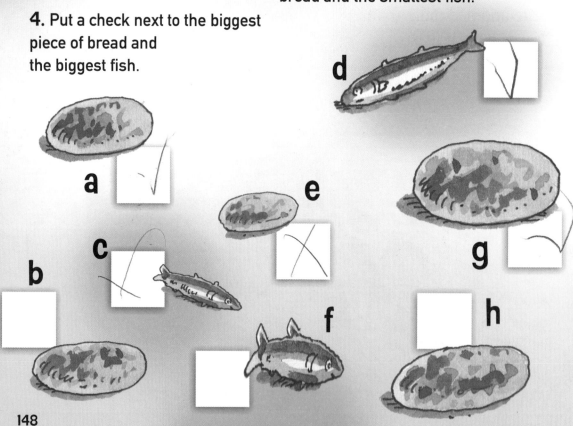

a

b

c

d

e

f

g

h

148

ADD COLOR

Color the picture.

The Good Neighbor

Luke 10:25–37

"Love God with all your heart," said Jesus. "Love your neighbor as much as you love yourself!" said Jesus.

"But who is my neighbor?" asked a man.

To answer the question, Jesus told the man this story.

"A man was once traveling down the road from Jerusalem to Jericho when he was attacked by robbers.

They took his money and his clothes and hurt him so badly that he couldn't move. He lay beside the road in the heat of the day for hours and hours. He was sure he would die if no one came to help him.

"Then a man came toward him.

"'At last!' thought the injured man. 'Help has come!' But the traveler walked on past as if he hadn't even noticed the injured man.

"Another man approached. 'Surely this man will help me!' thought the man, his head throbbing with pain. But the second man walked past him too and pretended he couldn't see him at all.

"'Now I must surely die!' wailed the man. The sun was beating down on his wounded head.

"Just then a third man, a Samaritan, came down the road. As

soon as he saw the wounded man, he rushed up to him.

"'What happened to you?' he asked. 'Let me help you.'

"The Samaritan gave the man something to drink, bandaged his wounds, and lifted him on the back of his own donkey. He took the man to an inn, where the Samaritan paid the innkeeper two silver coins to look after him.

"'Look after him,' he told the innkeeper. 'If he costs you any more than this, I will pay you when I return.'

"Now," said Jesus. "Who was the poor man's neighbor?"

"The one who was kind to him," replied the man.

"Yes. Go and do the same," said Jesus.

SPOT the DIFFERENCES

Find and check the picture that matches the picture in the yellow box. All the other pictures have one difference. Find and circle each of these changes.

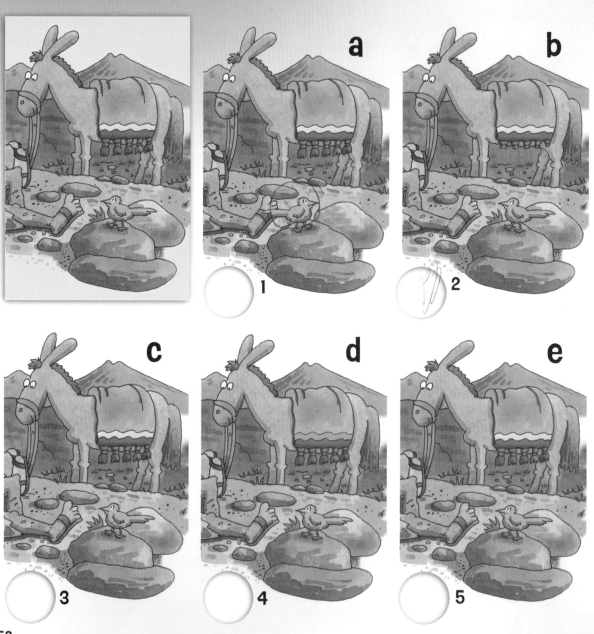

COPY the WORD

Donkey

CONNECT the DOTS

Who was watching the good neighbor help the injured man?
Connect the dots, and color in the picture.

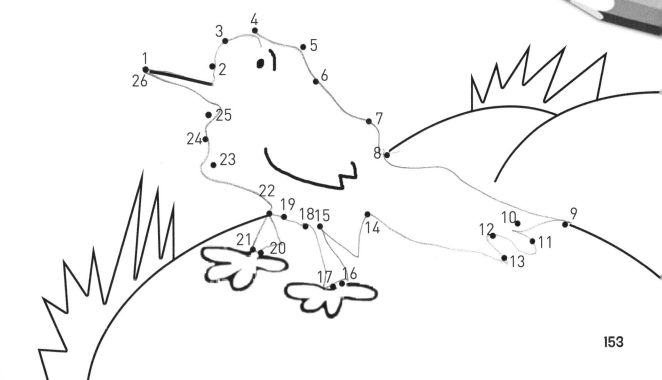

The Story of the Lost Sheep

Luke 15:3–7

Jesus once told this story about a shepherd:

"A shepherd once had a hundred sheep. He knew them all and looked after them very well. If wild animals came close, the shepherd chased them away. He did everything he could to protect his sheep.

"One day, the shepherd counted his sheep and found that one was missing! Where could it be?

"He set out from the sheepfold to look for the lost sheep. He left the other ninety-nine safely penned in the fold.

"The shepherd looked everywhere: behind bushes, near the stream, behind rocks, and in craggy places. There was no sign of the missing sheep.

"Suddenly there came a faint bleating sound. Was it the lost sheep?

"Yes! The shepherd had found his lost sheep at last.

"Gently, the shepherd put the lost sheep on his shoulders and carried it carefully home to the sheepfold.

"He was so pleased to find his lost sheep that he held a party and invited all his neighbors. They knew how much he loved his sheep.

"God is a bit like that shepherd," said Jesus. "He cares if any one of His sheep is lost. The angels in heaven rejoice and sing when anyone on earth tells God that he is sorry for the wrong things he has done."

155

COUNT the SHEEP

1. How many sheep can you count in this picture?

2. How many sheep ears can you see?

3. How many sheep legs can you see?

156

MAZE

Help the shepherd return to the rest of the flock.

The Man Who Could Not See

Luke 18:35–43

A poor blind man had been sitting at the roadside every day of his life. He listened for the sound of a coin or two clinking in his begging bowl. But today none came. Where was everybody? He could hear crowds

of people going past, but nobody stopped.

He heard a name. "Jesus! Let's see Jesus! Jesus can heal people!"

The man, who was called Bartimaeus, got to his feet.

"Jesus! Take pity on me!" he shouted as loudly as he possibly could.

"Be quiet, blind man!" grumbled people in the crowd.

"Bring the blind man to me," Jesus said firmly. "What do you want Me to do for you?" asked Jesus kindly.

"I want to see!" the blind man sighed.

"Then see!" said Jesus. "You believe I can help you. Your faith has made you well!"

All at once, the man's eyes became bright and clear and the world was full of color and movement.

"Thanks be to God!" shouted the man. "I can see! I can see!"

The crowd saw what had happened and joined Bartimaeus in praising God for the wonderful thing Jesus had done.

FIND and COUNT

1. One of the people opposite isn't in the crowd who saw the blind man made well. Write their letter in the box.

2. How many children can you see in the crowd?

3. How many grown-ups can you see in the crowd?

4. How many people are wearing green head coverings?

5. How many people are wearing a pink belt?

FIND the DIFFERENCES

Find ten differences between these two pictures and circle them.

The Little Tax Collector

Luke 19:1–10

Zacchaeus was a tax collector. No one liked him. In fact he had cheated many people and stolen money. He was not a popular man at all.

One day, Jesus was passing through Jericho, and Zacchaeus wanted to see Him. He had heard great things about Jesus and wanted to see Him with his own eyes.

Crowds of people lined the streets. Zacchaeus was very short, however, and could not hope to see Jesus unless he was above the crowd. He spotted a sycamore tree.

"I'll climb that tree!" said Zacchaeus to himself. "If I can sit above the crowd, I ought to be able to see Jesus when He comes past."

He didn't have to wait long. Jesus was on His way!

As Jesus came close, Zacchaeus leaned out of the branches to get a good look. Jesus was coming! Then suddenly Zacchaeus nearly fell out of the tree in amazement! Jesus had stopped beneath the tree and was calling up to him in the branches!

"Zacchaeus, hurry down!" said Jesus, "I must stay and eat at your house today."

Zacchaeus climbed down and greeted Jesus with great joy. He could hardly believe it. Why would Jesus want to speak to him? Nobody else ever did!

"You are most welcome in my house," said Zacchaeus.

Zacchaeus was a changed man. He later told Jesus, "I will give half of all I own to the poor. If I have cheated anyone, I will pay him back four times as much."

He kept his word.

"The Son of Man came to find and to save the lost," said Jesus. "This man has come to God's kingdom."

WHERE ARE THEY?

How many birds are hiding in the tree?

ODD ONE OUT

a   b   c

Which of these pictures is different from the others?

COLORS

The people are wearing colorful clothes. Draw a line to show:

A lady with a yellow robe

A man with a green headdress

A man in a brown coat

A man with a blue belt

A man with a red turban

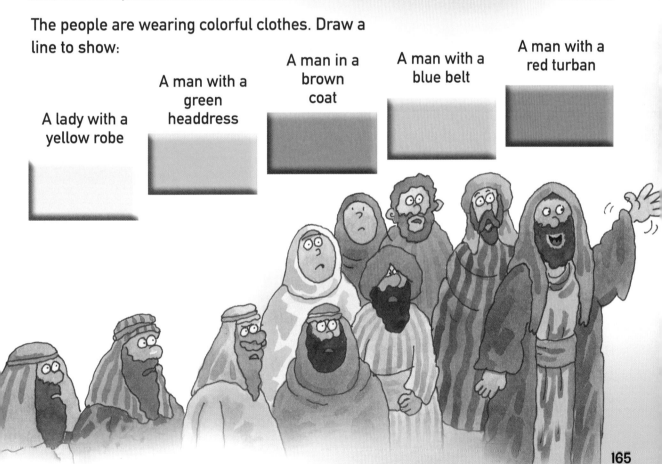

The King on a Donkey

Matthew 21:1–11

It was time for the Passover festival when people remembered the time God had rescued Moses and the Israelites from slavery in Egypt.

Jesus spent a few days with His friends Martha, Mary, and Lazarus in Bethany. Then He set off for the city of Jerusalem.

Jesus sent two friends ahead of Him. "Go to the village over there. You will find a young donkey that has never been ridden before. Bring it to Me. If the owner asks what you are doing, tell him that your Master needs it."

They went to the village and saw the young donkey. They were just untying it when the owner

said, "What are you doing with my donkey?"

"The Master needs it!" they said.

The friends took the donkey to Jesus and put their cloaks on the donkey's back. Then Jesus rode into Jerusalem.

Great crowds of people cheered for Jesus and waved palm branches and spread their cloaks on the road.

"Hosanna!" they cried in a loud voice. "God bless the King who comes in the name of the Lord!"

NUMBER the BOXES

Number the boxes below to remake the picture.

WHAT GOES WHERE?

Jesus Dies on the Cross

Luke 22:14–22; John 13:1–17; 19:1–42

Jesus had many friends, but He also had enemies. They wanted to get rid of Him. Jesus knew that He was going to die. He shared one last special meal with His disciples and washed their feet to show them they must take care of one another.

Jesus took a cup of wine, gave thanks to God, and passed it around to His friends. "Take this and drink," He said to them.

Then Jesus took a piece of bread, broke it and gave it to the others, saying, "This is My body, given for you. Do this and remember Me."

Jesus' friends didn't understand what Jesus meant. They didn't understand when He told them He would soon be going away from them.

Judas Iscariot, one of Jesus' friends, betrayed Him, and soldiers came to arrest Him. They were cruel to Him, beat Him, and made Him wear a purple robe. They put a crown of thorns on His head.

"People call You a king!" they mocked.

Jesus had to carry a heavy cross to a hill called Golgotha. Two criminals were going to be put on crosses next to Jesus. But Jesus had done nothing wrong.

Above His head was a sign saying: **King of the Jews.**

Jesus' mother, Mary, and His best friends stood close by and watched. They hated to see Him suffering.

Jesus was put on a cross and left to die.

Darkness covered the land. At the ninth hour, Jesus cried out to God in a loud voice. Then He died. A soldier put a sword in His side to make sure.

Jesus' body was taken down from the cross and put in a tomb in the rock. A large stone was rolled across the door of the tomb.

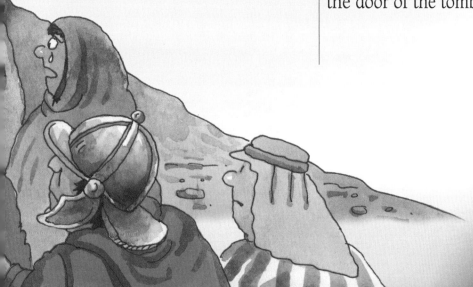

MATCH the PAIRS

Draw a line to join the helmets that are
exactly the same.

FIND the CROSSES

Color in the shapes with a dot. Use lots of colors to create a stained-glass window.

How many crosses can you find?

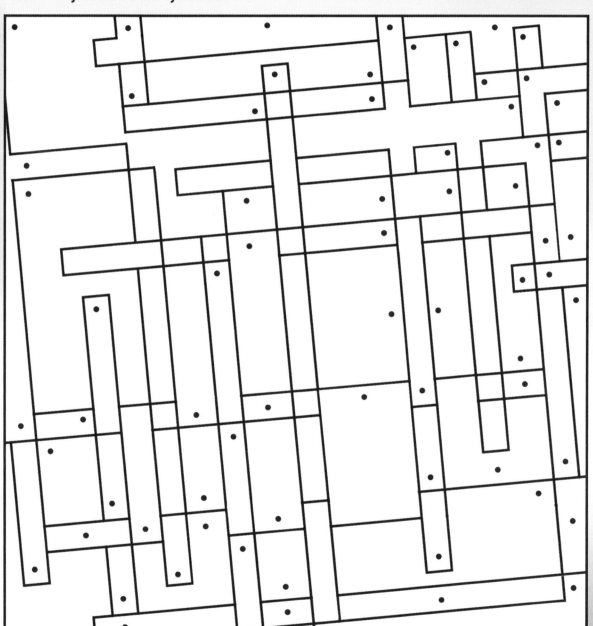

Jesus Is Alive

Luke 22:14–22; John 13:1–17; 19:1–42; 20:19

Three days had passed since Jesus had died on the cross.

Jesus' disciples were terribly sad. Their friend and Master had left them.

Other people were sad too, including a group of women.

On the third day, the women went to visit the tomb. They took herbs and spices to put on Jesus' body. That was the custom in those days when someone had died.

But when the women reached the tomb, they had a big shock! They found that the heavy stone had been rolled away from the entrance.

The women were afraid. They looked into the tomb. The body was gone! Where was Jesus? Who had taken Him?

Suddenly, two men in bright shining clothes appeared at the entrance.

The women bowed down to the ground, full of fear and trembling. Then the men spoke to the women, saying, "Why are you looking for Jesus here? He is not dead, He is alive! Remember what He told you before He left you?"

The women tried to remember. Jesus had said many things they didn't understand. He had said He was leaving them, but yes, He had said He would come back! Could it really be true?

The women ran to tell the disciples as fast as they could.

"Jesus is alive!" they said. "The tomb is empty!"

The disciples did not believe the women. Peter ran to the tomb to see for himself. He saw the cloths that Jesus' body had been wrapped in, but sure enough, Jesus was not there!

Then Jesus Himself came and spoke to Mary. She saw Him for herself! Not long afterward, Jesus appeared to His disciples too, and they knew that Jesus really was alive again!

MISSING LETTERS

Fill in the missing letters to see what the women told the disciples.

J_e_s_u_s _i_s _a_l_i_v_e!

BIG and SMALL

Put a **B** next to the biggest jar and an **S** next to the smallest one.

a

d

e

g

B b

h

S c

f

FIND and COUNT

Look at the picture below, and find and count how
many of these creatures you can find.

 1 $\boxed{4}$

 2 $\boxed{1}$

 3 $\boxed{5}$

Which creature appears
the most times in
the picture? $\boxed{C}$

Which creature appears the
least number
of times? $\boxed{B}$

 a

 b

c

Thomas Believes

John 20:19–29

It was late on Sunday evening when Jesus appeared to His disciples. They were meeting in a room in town and had locked the doors tightly. They were afraid they might be arrested because they were friends of Jesus.

Suddenly Jesus was there in the room with them.

"Peace be with you," He said. He showed them the wounds in His hands and His side. There was no doubt about it. This was Jesus!

Thomas was not there that day.

When his friends told him the good news, he could not believe it.

"But we have seen Him!" said his friends.

"Well, unless I can see His hands and feet and the marks where He was nailed to the cross, I won't believe it," answered Thomas.

A week later, Thomas and all the disciples were gathered together and had locked all the doors.

Suddenly, Jesus was there in the room with them! "Peace be with you," said Jesus. Then He turned to Thomas and said, "Put your finger in the wounds in My hands and your hand in My side. Stop doubting, Thomas, and believe!"

Thomas answered, "My Lord and my God!"

"You believe because you have seen Me," said Jesus. "How happy will people be when they believe without seeing Me for themselves."

SPOT the DIFFERENCES And Apple

The pictures outside the box all have one detail that is different from the one inside. Mark each difference with a circle.

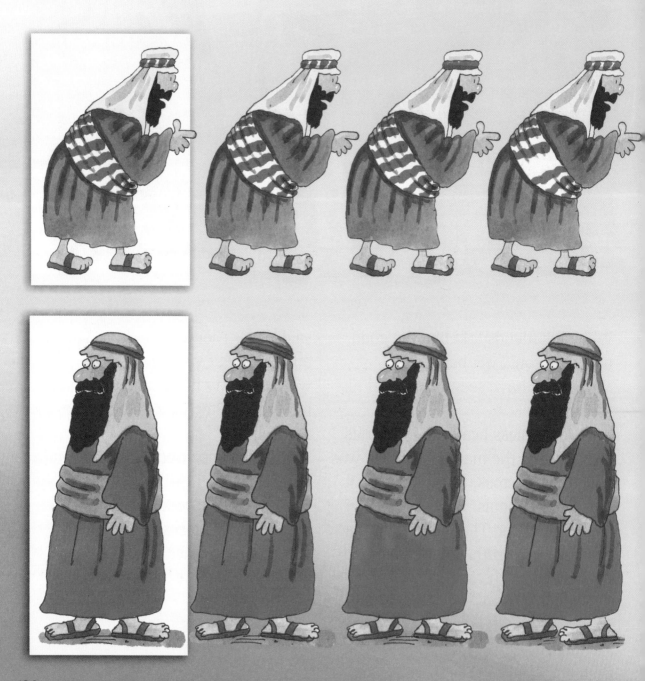

WHOSE HAND?

Write the number that identifies each hand from the main picture in the space next to the correct detail.

a

b

c

d

e

Breakfast on the Beach

John 21:1–14

Jesus appeared to His disciples early one morning. This is what happened:

Peter wanted to go out fishing.

"I'm setting off now," he told his friends. "Does anyone want to come fishing with me?"

Six other disciples joined him, and they pushed the boat out on to the lake. It was still early in the morning. They put their nets in the water and waited for the fish to come. But nothing happened. They did not catch a single fish.

Peter looked up and saw a figure on the beach. They couldn't see who it was. The man called to Peter.

"Throw your net on the other side of the boat, and you will catch plenty of fish," said the man.

So the disciples threw their nets on the other side. At once the net became so full of fish that the fishermen could not pull it into the boat!

Suddenly one of the disciples knew who the man on the shore must be. It had to be Jesus!

They went to the shore and saw a charcoal fire there with some fish and some bread.

Jesus told them to bring some of the fresh fish to cook. "Come and eat!" He said.

The disciples were very happy to see Jesus again!

MISSING PIECES

Can you show where each of these fragments fits in the picture below? Write the correct letter into each white empty space.

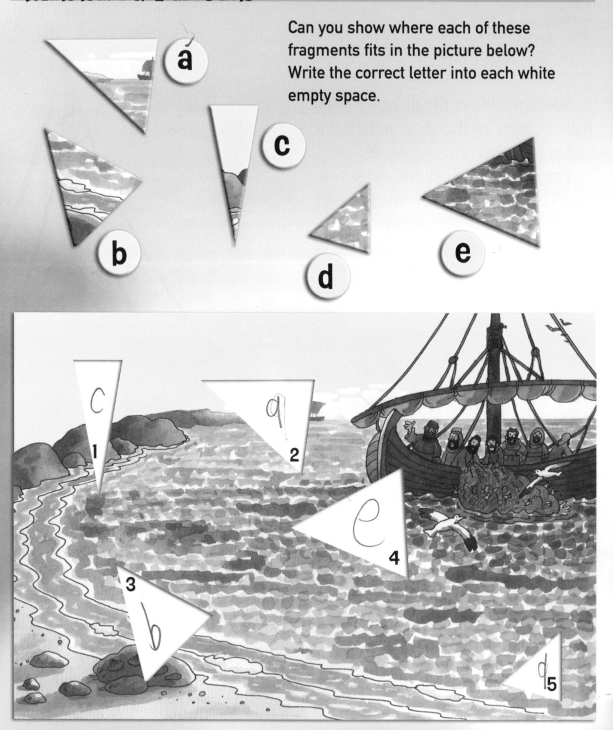

WORD SEARCH

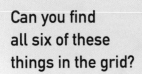

Can you find
all six of these
things in the grid?

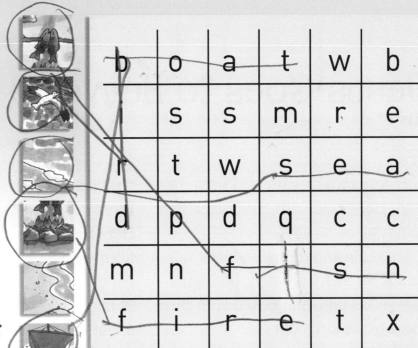

b	o	a	t	w	b
i	s	s	m	r	e
r	t	w	s	e	a
d	p	d	q	c	c
m	n	f	i	s	h
f	i	r	e	t	x

COUNTING PUZZLE

How many seagulls can you
count in the picture?

185

Jesus Goes to Heaven

Acts 1:1–14

After Jesus was resurrected from the dead, He stayed with His disciples for 40 days.

Jesus ate and drank with His friends on many different occasions during this time and talked with them about God's kingdom.

When they met together, Jesus told His disciples something very important that they must do.

"Don't leave Jerusalem," He said, "but wait for the special gift that I will leave you. You must wait for God's Holy Spirit to come. Then you will be filled with power and will be able to tell everyone about Me. You will want to make sure everyone knows about the things I have taught you, and about My death and resurrection, wherever they live in the world."

Jesus' disciples asked Him many questions. They wanted to know if God's kingdom was coming soon.

"Don't worry about these things," said Jesus. "You don't need to know the times or places for them."

Then Jesus was taken up to heaven. A cloud hid Him from their sight as they watched.

Jesus' friends were still watching the sky when two men appeared next to them. They were dressed all in white.

"Why are you standing here looking up at the sky?" they asked. "Jesus will come back again in the same way as you saw Him go," they promised.

Jesus' friends believed all that Jesus had told them. They waited in Jerusalem for the Holy Spirit, praying together.

They knew each other well. There was Peter, John, James and Andrew, Philip and Thomas, Bartholomew and Matthew, James, Simon, and Judas. They chose another disciple, called Matthias, to replace Judas Iscariot who had betrayed Jesus.

Mary, Jesus' mother, and other women who loved Jesus, joined them to pray to God. About 120 people believed in Jesus at that time.

PICTURE MAZE

Can you help the group of people find their way to Jerusalem?

SPOT the DIFFERENCES

Find eight differences between these two pictures,
and mark them with a circle.

The Good News of Jesus

Acts 2:1–47

On the day of Pentecost, Jesus' disciples and all the other believers were meeting together in a room.

Suddenly there was a noise like a strong wind blowing. The noise filled the whole house. Tongues of fire touched everyone in the room, and everyone was filled with the Holy Spirit.

It was just as Jesus had promised. The believers found they could suddenly speak in all kinds of languages! Many people in Jerusalem from other countries could understand what they were saying.

Peter told the crowds all about Jesus. He told them about how Jesus had done amazing things, healed people, and shown God's power. Jesus had been put to death on a cross, but He had come alive again!

"Turn away from doing wrong," said Peter. "Believe in Jesus and be baptized. You will be forgiven, and you will receive God's gift of the Holy Spirit!"

About three thousand people believed and were baptized that same day and joined the disciples.

Jesus' friends and the new believers wanted to tell more people the good news.

Some believers traveled to other countries, many faced great danger, and some never came home again. But they were all filled with God's love for the people they met.

They wanted to share the good news of Jesus and tell everyone about God's wonderful kingdom.

MISSING LETTERS

Fill in the missing letters to complete the message the disciples gave to the crowds.

"I b___g y__ ___d n___!"

WHAT'S WRONG?

Can you find eight mistakes in the picture below?
Mark them with a circle.

COLORS

1. How many people are wearing something that is bright yellow?

2. How many people are wearing something that is blue?

3. How many people are wearing something that is green?

COLOR LINKS

Draw a line from each block of color to something the same color in the picture below.

red

blue

orange

green

yellow

The Power of the Holy Spirit

Acts 2:1–12; 3:1–10

Jesus had died. But God had brought Him back to life—and now He would never die again. It was a miracle.

When the Holy Spirit came to help the people at Pentecost, all those who had been friends of Jesus wanted to tell everyone the good news.

"Tell God you are sorry for all the bad things you've done," Peter told a huge crowd. "Jesus welcomes anyone who wants to be God's friend."

More than 3,000 people became friends of Jesus that day. Soon they were known as Christians. They shared everything they owned. Day by day, more people believed and joined them.

Jesus' friends were also able to heal people just as Jesus had done. When Peter and John went to the temple to pray, they met a man there begging because he couldn't walk.

"We don't have any money," Peter said, "but Jesus has given us power to help you walk. Stand up!"

The man stood and walked.

"God is great! Look, I can walk!" The man told everyone what had happened to him.

195

WHAT'S in the CROWD?

1. Which crowd has the most sticks?

2. Which crowd contains the most children?

3. Which crowd contains a lady with a pot on her head?

4. Which crowd contains a dog?

5. Where is the little green snake and rabbit?

6. Which crowd is the largest?

COMPLETE the PICTURE

Draw the bodies of the two men.

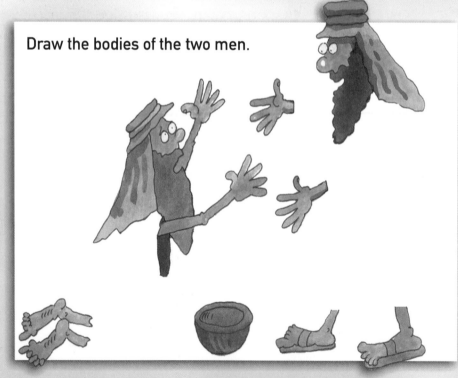

A

B

C

Saul Meets Jesus

Acts 9:1–25

A man called Saul hated the new Christians. He searched them out so they could be put in prison.

On his way to Damascus, Saul was blinded by a bright light.

"Saul, Saul," said a voice, "why are you attacking Me?"

"Who are You?" Saul asked.

"I am Jesus," He replied. "When you hurt My friends, you hurt Me too. But I have something important for you to do. Go into the city, and you will find out what it is."

Saul's friends led him into Damascus, where a man called Ananias came to see him.

"Jesus has sent me to help you see again," Ananias told Saul.

Then Saul's life was completely changed. He received the Holy Spirit and was baptized. Now he was called Paul.

But when the
religious leaders
heard what had
happened, they
planned to kill
Paul. His friends
helped him escape
in a basket from
a window in the
city walls.

199

WHAT'S WRONG

There are three things wrong in this picture. Draw a circle around each one.

WORD SEARCH

Can you find these four words?

basket   window
rope   Paul

```
I  J  K  R  I
A  H  S  O  W
B  P  B  V  I
W  A  A  C  N
B  A  S  K  D
F  O  K  E  O
S  B  E  U  W
P  A  T  P  I
B  S  R  A  R
I  I  C  U  F
W  Y  U  L  D
E  R  O  P  E
```

SPOT the BLOCK

Label each
picture block
A, B, C, D, or **E.**

1 P   2 A   3 D   4 C   5 D

SPOT and COUNT

In the picture there are eight __ .   **P**__ __ __ __ __

In the picture there is one __ .   **B**__ __ __ __ __

In the picture there are three __ .   **W**__ __ __ __ __ __

Philip and the Man in the Chariot

Acts 8:26–39

The new Christians all found that their lives had changed.

Philip was told by an angel to go to Gaza where he would find a man sitting in a chariot. Philip found the man reading from a scroll. The Holy Spirit told Philip to help the man.

"Can you explain this prophecy from the prophet Isaiah to me?" the man asked Philip.

"It's about someone who has died."

Philip began to tell the man all about Jesus: how He had been crucified and raised from the dead by a miracle—and how all His friends had received power to live as new people.

"Here's a stream of water so you can baptize me," said the man. "I want to be a Christian too."

The chariot stopped, and Philip baptized the man in the water. Then the man returned to his home in Ethiopia, ready to tell everyone there about Jesus too.

GO to GAZA

Find your way to the man in the chariot.

Start here

Congratulations!
You have arrived.

205

Cornelius, the Soldier Who Loved God

Acts 10:1–48

Cornelius was a Roman soldier. He loved God and was always ready to help anyone. One day an angel came to him.

"God has seen what a good man you are, Cornelius. He wants you to meet Peter, who is staying in Joppa."

Cornelius was amazed by the angel—but he sent his men to fetch Peter. Meanwhile God spoke to Peter in a vision. Peter saw a blanket, filled with every kind of creature.

"Have something to eat, Peter," said a voice.

"But we are not allowed these foods," said Peter.

"God has made them good," said the voice. "It's okay to eat them."

Then Peter heard someone knocking at the door.

"Captain Cornelius welcomes you to his house," the men told Peter.

So Peter went to meet Cornelius. Then he understood what God was telling him. All people were welcome to be part of God's family, people from every nation on earth. Peter told Cornelius and the other people there about Jesus—and they were baptized.

A ROMAN SOLDIER'S WEAPONS

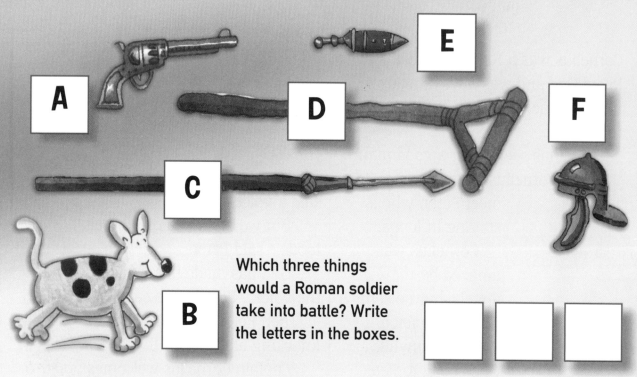

A

E

D

F

C

B

Which three things would a Roman soldier take into battle? Write the letters in the boxes.

LOTS of ANIMALS

Peter saw a vision of lots of animals. How many animals can you find in the grid below?

```
C O W R I M O U S E E D H
A I W P G O A T N S K U O
T C H I C K E N W P A C R
I D O G U L G F I S H K S
D E E R C E A G L E N E E
```

COPY CAT DOG

Copy the dog using the grid to help you.

WHAT'S WRONG?

Find one thing wrong with each of the Roman soldiers.

People Pray for Peter

Acts 12:6–19

People who knew Jesus could not stop telling others about Him.

But it was dangerous to be a Christian. James, one of the first disciples, was executed. Peter was put in prison. King Herod planned a public trial, hoping to stop other people from becoming Christians. He made sure Peter was heavily guarded and chained between two soldiers.

Peter's friends were worried about what would happen to him. They prayed that God would help him.

That night, God sent an angel to the prison cell.

"Quickly!" said the angel. "Wake up, put on your shoes, and wrap your cloak around you."

Peter watched with amazement as the chains fell off his wrists, and the doors opened and closed! He left the soldiers sleeping and followed

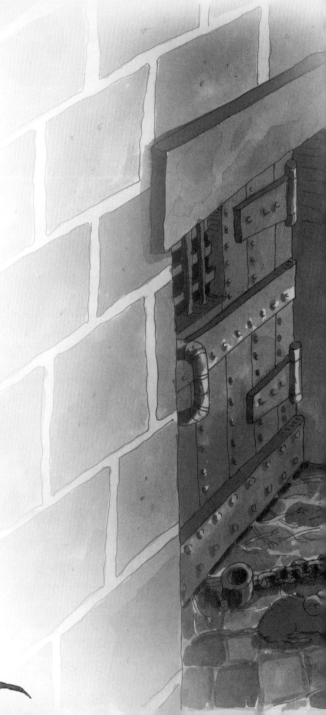

the angel into the street. He went to his friends' house and banged on the door.

God had answered their prayers! Peter was safe and with them again.

SPOT the SPELLING MISTAKES

Can you find all six spelling mistakes?

It was dungerous to be a Christian. James, one of the first disksiples, was executed. Peter was put in prison. Kinn Herod planned a public trial, hopping to stop other people from becoming Christians. He mad sure Peter was heavily guarded and chained between two soldiures.

SPOT the DIFFERENCE

Can you spot all six differences between these two pictures?

Draw a line to each of the six changes.

CAN YOU REMEMBER?

Who was executed?

1. J __ __ __ __

Herod was a ____ .

3. K __ __ __

What did God send to the prison?

2. A __ __ __ __

What fell from the wrists of Peter?

4. C __ __ __ __ __

What did God hear and answer?

5. P __ __ __ __ __ __

1 2 3 4 5 6

The Storm and the Shipwreck

Acts 27:1–44; 28:1–31

Paul used every chance he had to tell other people about Jesus. Wherever he went, people became Christians. But sometimes he was beaten and put in prison.

When he was sent to Rome to stand trial, Paul's ship ran into a terrible storm and was wrecked off the coast of Malta. The passengers swam to the shore or drifted in, clinging to the wreckage. Even during the three months they stayed there, Paul was able to heal many people.

Paul was put under house arrest in Rome with a soldier to guard him. He spent the next two years telling the Romans about Jesus and writing to the new churches, reminding everyone that they should take care of each other and treat other people well.

The disciples had done what Jesus asked them to. The Christian church began with them and spread all over the world.

ALL IN ORDER

Write 1–5 in the boxes to put the picture strips in the correct order.

WHERE?

1. Where was Paul sailing?

R _ _ _ _

2. What island was Paul's ship wrecked on?

M _ _ _ _ _

A Vision of Heaven

Revelation

John was imprisoned on the island of Patmos. But Jesus had not forgotten him. Jesus spoke to him there in a vision, giving him messages for all the churches. Jesus was not like the carpenter John had known years ago—He looked like God, shining like the sun—and John fell to his knees and worshipped Him.

"I am the beginning and the end," said Jesus. "I was dead, but now I am alive, and I will never die again."

Jesus encouraged Christians to be brave—even when people treated them badly because they trusted Him. The time would come when good would overcome evil and everyone who had suffered would live with God forever in a beautiful new world.

"Soon there will be no more pain or suffering, no more death and dying, no more tears or sadness," said Jesus. "Anyone who comes to Me will be forgiven and will live with Me in heaven forever."

NOT FOUND in HEAVEN

Move one letter in each word to find something that will not exist in heaven.

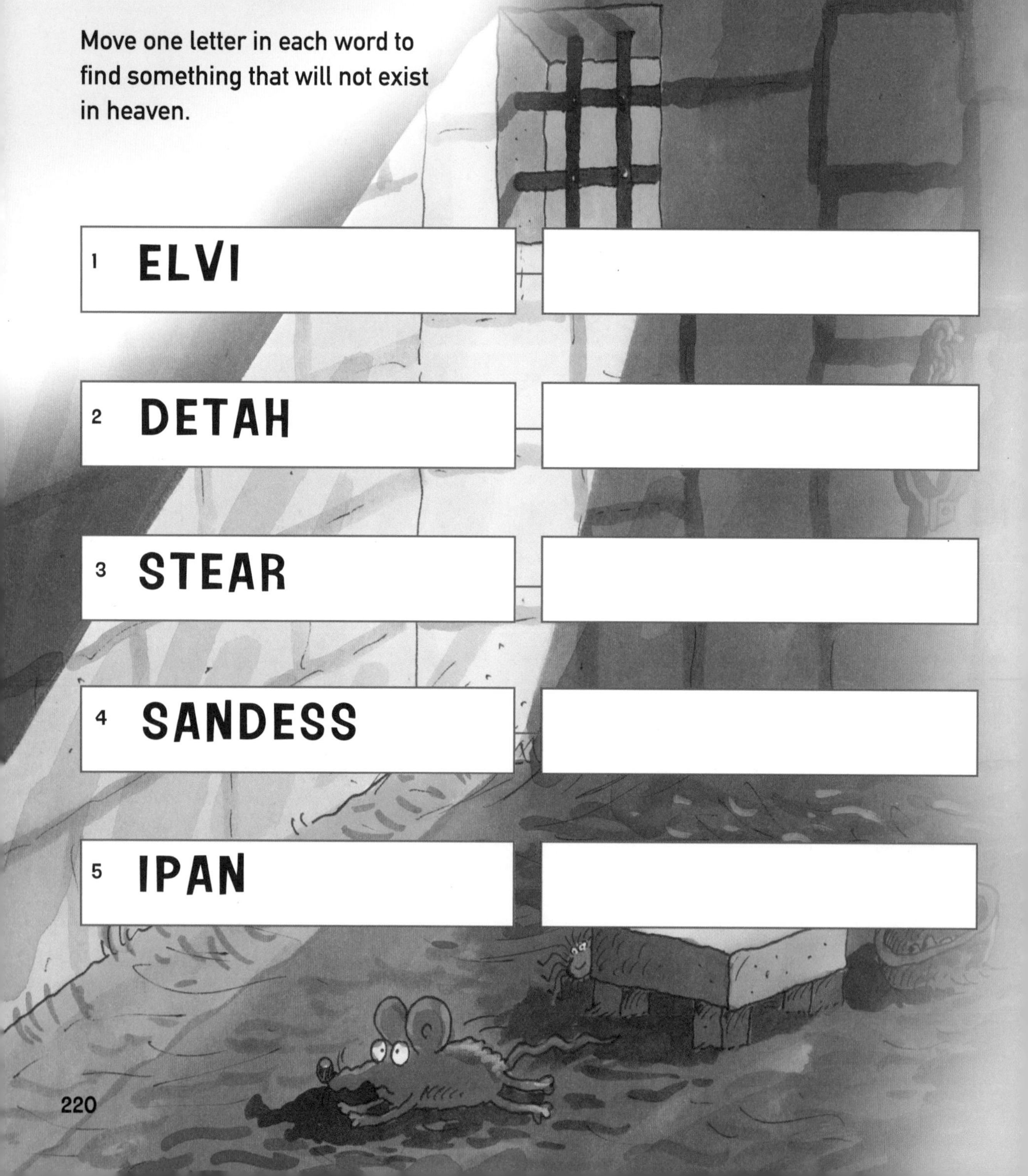

1 **ELVI**

2 **DETAH**

3 **STEAR**

4 **SANDESS**

5 **IPAN**

BUILD the PICTURE

Re-create this picture by putting the squares in the right place.

Write the letter of the correct square in the grid below.

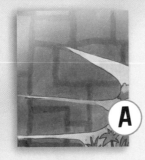
A

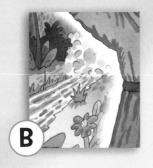
B

C

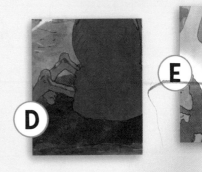
D · E

F · G

H · I

1 F	2 H	3 E
4 A	5	6
7	8	9

New Testament Puzzle Solutions

Page 105

There are 5 mice in the picture.

a 4; b 2; c 3; d 1

Page 108

Page 109

There are 6 goats.

Page 112

Page 113

Page 116

Round shapes: 4 and 6;
Square shapes: 1 and 3;
Triangular shapes: 2 and 5.

Page 117

1: 3; 2: 2; 3: 4; 4: 9

Page 120

Page 121

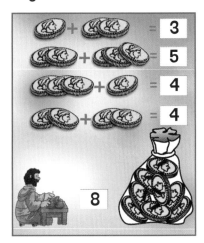

Page 124

Attached rope: 6

Page 125

Page 128

1 False; 2 False; 3 False;
4 True.

Page 129

Page 132

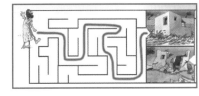

Page 133

Page 136

a, d, e, f.

Page 137

s	t	o	r	m	v
m	o	c	a	l	m
r	s	w	i	n	d
a	w	a	v	e	s
i	w	a	t	e	r
n	c	k	a	m	s

Calm is the opposite of **storm**.

Page 140

Page 141

Page 148

1: 5; 2: 3; 3 f.

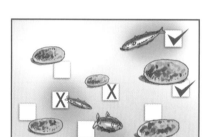

Page 156

1: 11; 2: 20; 3 9.

Page 157

Page 144

Page 152

Page 160

1: b; 2: 2; 3: 17; 4: 5; 5: 1.

Page 145

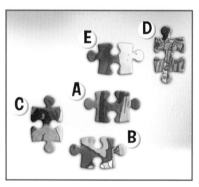

Page 153

Donkey

Page 161

Page 164

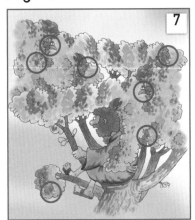

Page 165

1 a is the odd picture.

Page 168

Page 169

Page 172

Page 173

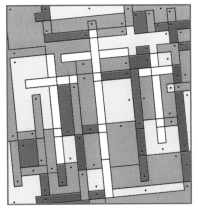

Page 176

Jesus is alive!

Biggest: C; Smallest: A

Page 177

1: 4; 2: 1; 3: 5

1 Dragonflies; 2 Butterflies.

Page 180

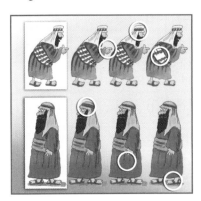

Page 181

225

Page 184

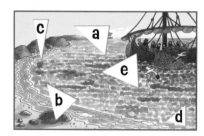

Page 185

b	o	a	t	w	b
i	s	s	m	r	e
r	t	w	s	e	a
d	p	d	q	c	c
m	n	f	i	s	h
f	i	r	e	t	x

Page 188

Page 189

Page 192

I bring you good news!

Page 193

1: 4; 2: 6; 3: 7.

Page 196

1: C; 2: B; 3: C; 4: A; 5: A;
6: B.

Page 200

I J K R I
A H S O W
B P B V I
W A A C N
B A S K D
F O E E O
S B T U W
P A R P I
B S C A R
I I U U F
W Y R L D
E R O P E

Page 201

1: 8 people; 2: 1 basket;
3: 3 windows.

Page 204-205

Page 217

1 Rome; 2 Malta.

Page 208

A Roman soldier would take:
E,C and F.

There are 8 animals in the wordsearch.

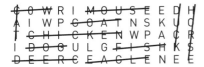

Page 212

Page 220

1 evil; 2 death; 3 tears;
4 sadness; 5 pain.

Page 221

Page 209

Page 213

1 Jesus; 2 an angel; 3 king;
4 chains; 5 prayers.